S0-AUL-343

Vietnam in Prose and Film

ST. JOSEPH'S COLLEGE LIBRARY
P.O. Box 7009
Mt. View, CA 94039

113057

James C. Wilson

VIETNAM IN PROSE AND FILM

McKEON MEMORIAL LIBRARY
ST. PATRICK'S SEMINARY
320 MIDDLEFIELD ROAD
MENLO PARK, CALIFORNIA 94025

ST. JOSEPH'S COLLEGE LIBRARY
P.O. Box 7009
Mt. View, CA 94039

DISCARD

Jefferson, N.C.   London
McFarland & Company, Inc., Publishers
1982

P
92
.U5
W53
1982

810.9358
W694

Epigraph (opposite) from Hugh Selwyn Mauberly *by*
Ezra Pound; from Personae, *copyright* © *1926*
by Ezra Pound; reprinted by permission of New
Directions Pub. Corp.
Passages from Dispatches *are copyright* © *1977 by Michael*
Herr; reprinted by permission of Alfred A. Knopf, Inc.

Library of Congress Cataloging in Publication Data

Wilson, James, 1948-
  Vietnam in prose and film.

  Includes bibliographies and index.
  1. Mass media — United States. 2. Vietnam Conflict,
1961-1975 — Literature and the war. 3. Vietnamese Conflict,
1961-1975, in motion pictures. I. Title.
P92.U5W53   302.2'34'0973   82-6635
                    AACR2
ISBN 0-89950-050-1

Copyright © 1982 by James C. Wilson

Manufactured in the United States of America

010441
FEB 20 '85

Died some, pro patria,
        non 'dulce' non 'et decor' …
walked eye-deep in hell
believing in old men's lies, then unbelieving
came home, home to a lie,
home to many deceits,
home to old lies and new infamy;
usury age-old and age-thick
and liars in public places.

> Ezra Pound
> *Hugh Selwyn Mauberly*

Table of Contents

Chronology of Events   vii

1. Introduction   1

2. A First Warning
   The Quiet American   8

3. Official Distortions 1950-1975
   "No Exit onto Reality"   15

4. Media Distortions
   "History's Heavy Attrition"   28

  5. Literary Distortions
        The Green Berets, et al.   36

  6. The Dope and Dementia Theory
        Dispatches and Other Evasions   43

  7. Recovering a Secret History
        One Very Hot Day and *Going After Cacciato*   53

  8. Moral Explorations
        The Prisoners of Quai Dong and *Dog Soldiers*   61

  9. Casualties
        The Pepsi Generation. Throwaway People   70

 10. Derealizing Vietnam: Hollywood
        The Celluloid War   79

 11. Conclusion   97

     Chapter Notes   103

     Bibliography   113

     Filmography   121

     Index   127

Chronology of Events

1873	Francis Barnier, a French adventurer, attacks Hanoi and declares the Red River open to international trade. French dominion in Vietnam begins.
1890	Ho Chi Minh born.
1940	France falls in Second World War. Japan takes its place as the imperial power in Vietnam.
1941	Ho Chi Minh founds the Vietnam Independence League.
August 19, 1946	After the fall of Japan, Ho Chi Minh establishes the Democratic Republic of Vietnam in Hanoi.

December 1946   France attempts to reestablish control in Vietnam; its army returns to Hanoi. Ho and his followers, the Viet Minh, become a guerrilla army. The first Indochina war begins.

1950   The United States begins to subsidize the French presence in Vietnam. President Truman sends a 35-man military aid group. Diem visits the United States and meets John F. Kennedy.

1954   The United States supplies 80 percent of French war expenditures in Vietnam. While urging that they continue the war, John Foster Dulles tells France the United States will not commit its own troops.

May 7, 1954   The Viet Minh, under the command of General Vo Nguyen Giap, defeat the French army at Dien Bien Phu. France can no longer continue the war.

June 1954   Colonel Edward G. Lansdale arrives in Saigon as head of the United States military mission and then as CIA chief of station for domestic affairs. Following orders to "beat the Geneva timetable of Communist take-over in the North," Lansdale's teams conduct sabotage and agit-prop work in both North and South Vietnam.

July 20, 1954   The Geneva Conference on Indochina declares a demilitarized zone at the 17th parallel. The Geneva Accords call for elections to be held in July 1956 to reunite Vietnam. The United States refuses to sign.

September 1954   John Foster Dulles creates the Southeast Asia Treaty Organization (SEATO).

1955   Diem, backed by the United States, repudiates the Geneva Accords and organizes the Republic of Vietnam as an independent nation, with himself as president. The United States arms seven divisions of South Vietnamese with American weapons.

1956   Elections called for by the Geneva Accords to reunite North and South Vietnam are not held.

May 1957　President Eisenhower receives Diem in Washington, where he is greeted as a hero.

December 1960　The National Liberation Front (NLF) is founded in South Vietnam.

1961　The United States build-up in South Vietnam begins. President Kennedy commits 16,000 advisers over the next two years to help defend South Vietnam. The second Indochina war begins.

June 16, 1963　Thich Quang Duc, a Buddhist bonze, burns himself to death in downtown Saigon, rallying Vietnamese Buddhists to resist Diem.

November 1, 1963　Diem is assassinated by military junta. The United States quickly recognizes the government of General Duong Van Minh in Saigon.

January 30, 1964　General Nguyen Kahn seizes the general staff headquarters in Saigon and proclaims himself chairman of the Military Revolutionary Council. Kahn wrests power from General Minh and the military junta. The United States immediately recognizes the government of General Kahn.

August 4, 1964　Gulf of Tonkin incident. President Johnson orders the bombing of North Vietnam.

March 1965　United States combat troops land at Da Nang. President Johnson begins massive bombing of North Vietnam.

June 1965　Generals Nguyen Kao Ky and Nguyen Van Thieu seize control of the Saigon government by military coup. General Ky is appointed chief of the executive committee.

1966　United States troop strength in Vietnam is at 200,000 by end of year. General Westmoreland begins "search and destroy" missions.

September 1967　General Thieu elected president of South Vietnam.

Fall 1967   United States troop strength is at 500,000.

January 31, 1968   The Tet Offensive. The NLF attack every major city in South Vietnam.

March 1968   The My Lai Massacre. President Johnson announces that he will not run for reelection and calls for peace talks with North Vietnam.

June 23, 1968   The Vietnam conflict becomes the longest war in United States history.

January 1969   United States troop strength reaches its peak at 542,000.

May 20, 1969   Peace talks begin in Paris.

July 8, 1969   President Nixon announces the first troop withdrawal from South Vietnam.

September 3, 1969   Ho Chi Minh dies.

April 30, 1970   President Nixon announces the invasion of Cambodia by United States and South Vietnamese troops.

February 1971   South Vietnamese troops, supported by United States air and medical units, invade Laos.

December 1972   The Christmas bombing of Hanoi.

January 25, 1973   A peace agreement is signed in Paris.

March 29, 1973   The last United States troops leave Vietnam.

April 30, 1975   South Vietnam surrenders to North Vietnam. Saigon becomes Ho Chi Minh City. Vietnam is reunited.

Chapter 1. Introduction

> *The war in Vietnam left a wound on my generation that hasn't healed. It has closed with the infection still raging inside. The longer that we ignore it the worse the infection grows.* — Mark Baker, *Nam*.

For the generation of Americans who came of age during the Vietnam War, the war "was what we had instead of happy childhoods," as Michael Herr writes in *Dispatches*.[1] We read about the war in every major newspaper and in every major magazine. We watched it every evening on the network news — images of American G.I.s firing into a treeline at an unseen enemy; images of napalm and white phosphorous igniting villages and jungles; images of orphans and refugees massed along the highways. We listened to all the progress reports, all the

1

promises of victory and lights at the end of the tunnels. As a nation we debated all the official reasons for the war — to contain communism, to defend freedom and democracy, to protect national security, to support our allies, to maintain American prestige. Meanwhile, Americans died in Vietnam for thirteen years, from 1961 through January 31, 1973. When it was over, the government of Saigon falling almost without a shot fired, 57,605 Americans had died and 303,700 had been wounded on Vietnamese soil.[2]

In April, 1975, after the last Americans had been evacuated from Saigon, President Gerald Ford proclaimed an end to the Vietnam "experience." Most Americans were eager to follow President Ford in relegating this nation's longest and most divisive war to the dustbin of history. After all, Vietnam had divided the nation, had estranged many of its citizens from their own government, and had led to a growing cynicism about government in general. Nearly everyone, whether for or against the war, found it painful to consider Vietnam in its aftermath: what we had done to Vietnam and the Vietnamese people was not pretty. And for what? The questions were too painful; many withdrew into the mute cynicism of the Watergate Era with an "I told you so" attitude as one debacle replaced another. Perhaps I.F. Stone best expressed this post-Vietnam cynicism when he wrote "every government is run by liars and thieves and nothing they say should be believed."[3]

By an unspoken agreement, the American people conspired to forget Vietnam. Peter Marin writes, in "Coming to Terms with Vietnam," that "what paralyzed us was not simply the guilt felt about Vietnam, but our inability to confront and comprehend that guilt: our refusal to face squarely what happened and why, and our unwillingness to determine, in the light of the past, our moral obligations for the future. In short, we spent a decade denying and evading guilt rather than using it to our advantage."[4] But, Marin argues, the moral quandaries remain, and in order to learn from our mistakes we must make an effort to break free from our silence and our cynicism.

Now, more than ever, we need to understand our debacle in Vietnam before a new spirit of militarization erases all memory of what happened there. Once again the rhetoric of intervention has become the currency of those who conduct our foreign policy. Walter LeFeber refers to these men as the "new revisionists" because of their efforts at "rewriting the record of failed military interventionism in the 1950 to 1975 era in order to build support for interventionsim in the 1980s."[5] Similarly, Noam Chomsky argues in *After the Cataclysm* that intellectuals and public officials alike are now engaged in an effort to "reconstruct recent history" in an attempt to salvage a "badly mauled imperial ideology."[6] The new revisionists point to the recent carnage in Indochina as a *"post hoc* justification for U.S. intervention by showing the awful consequences of its defeat."[7] No matter that the carnage resulted largely from the complete destruction of agrarian economies and the creation of millions of refugees driven into urban slums by an ever-widening war. By such convoluted logic, we deny a hundred years of Western imperialism and attribute the destruction of Indochina to the "evils of communism."

The new revisionists have been very successful in perpetuating their myths about the Vietnam conflict. For example, even such a sophisticated apologist for the war as Guenter Lewy can repeat the same platitudes that General Westmoreland used in his public speeches and memoirs. In his recent *America in Vietnam*, Lewy blames the loss of the war on the press, on public opinion, and on corrupt South Vietnamese. Lewy suggests that the United States might have won the war if the American government had intervened massively at an earlier date, and he even goes so far as to argue for a "moral justification" of the war, based on the erroneous assumption that the United States was stopping communist aggression from the North. Lewy conveniently fails to discuss how Vietnam came to be divided, North and South, or who it was that created the fictitious government in South Vietnam.

And what about the outcome of the war? Can the American defeat be so conveniently blamed on the press or the American public, who lacked the "will" to win the war? Despite the arguments of Lewy and other revisionists, the truth remains that the press by and large not only accepted but approved the government version of the war from 1954 at least until the 1968 Tet Offensive. In addition, the Vietnam War was a popular one, supported by the public and the great majority of elected public officials, as nearly every opinion poll taken during the 1960s demonstrated. Walter LeFeber reminds us that "the United States lost in Vietnam because Americans could not win the war without destroying what they were fighting to save — or, alternatively, without fighting for decades while surrendering those values at home and in the Western alliance for which the cold war was supposedly being waged."[8] And yet the myths persist, the most curious being that Vietnam was a noble cause in which we were betrayed by the venal South Vietnamese — a denial of twenty-one years of history.

All such myths need to be abandoned if we are to comprehend the war. To claim that it was too complicated, too surreal, too distorted by contending ideologies will no longer suffice. This claim is itself just another myth. In *Winners and Losers* Gloria Emerson comments that "it is easier to claim the war was impossible to understand, therefore Americans need not feel pain or guilt or the necessity to see themselves differently."[9] Emerson goes on to plead with her readers to remember the war in all of its detail: "it is important to remember, to spell the names correctly, to know the provinces, before we are persuaded that none of it happened, that none of us were in such places."[10]

In spite of what we would like to believe, the history of the Vietnam War is not inaccessible. The entire course of events has been recorded by French historians such as Paul Mus and Philippe Devillers, and by American historians such as Bernard Fall and Frances Fitzgerald. But we believe what we choose to believe, and we do not even choose to remember the hundreds of thousands of American deaths in the war nor the more than two million American veterans who came home as something less than heroes. They fought our war and they came home not to parades but to the indifference of their government, the incompetence of their veterans' hospitals, and the contempt of many of their fellow citizens.

More than any other war in American history, Vietnam was a class war, fought predominantly by minorities and the poor. Frances Fitzgerald writes in *Fire in the Lake* that Vietnam "was a white man's war being fought by blacks, a rich man's war being fought by the poor, an old man's war being fought by the young."[11] The soldiers who returned home to very much the same discrimination and the same poverty realized once again that they were "throwaway people," as Charles Durden writes in *No Bugles, No Drums* — the "ultimate luxury of a throwaway society."[12]

American losses in the Vietnam War speak clearly. In addition to the 57,605 dead, 519,000 Vietnam veterans have been officially classified as "disabled." Another 350,000 veterans received less than honorable discharges. The suffering of these men and their families cannot be measured or translated into statistics, of course, nor can the suffering of the families of the hundreds of thousands of draft resisters and deserters. Altogether the United States spent 165 billion dollars on military expenditures for the Vietnam War, but no one can calculate the long-term cost to the American economy. The effect of the war on how we see ourselves or how the rest of the world sees us as a people, may take years to determine.

Vietnamese losses were staggering. Too often we regard the war as an American tragedy, forgetting or disallowing the enormous suffering our nation inflicted upon the Vietnamese people. This attitude, prevalent in the political rhetoric of the war period, and in our current literature and cinema, reflects "the difficulty we have in seeing the reality of events, the justice of others' causes, or the suffering we inflict upon them,"[13] as Peter Marin suggests. Our self-absorption prevents us from acknowledging that we dropped 7,600,000 tons of bombs on North Vietnam, more than three times the total amount dropped during World War II. We do not acknowledge the more than 600,000 North and South Vietnamese soldiers, and the estimated 587,000 civilians, who died in the war. We do not acknowledge the three million civilians wounded and the nine million refugees generated by our "attriting" the base of Viet Cong support, which meant destroying the villages and fields. In the process of drying up the sea in which the Viet Cong swam, to use General Westmoreland's infamous metaphor, we defoliated 5.2 million acres of land with our Agent Orange and other chemicals. The old irony comes back to haunt us: we had to destroy Vietnam to save it, except that in the end nothing was saved, everything was lost.

For myself, I do not believe the war will disappear from memory. Too much was lost; too many of the generation growing up at the time had Vietnam instead of happy childhoods. Sooner or later, if those wounds are to be healed, we must come to some understanding of what happened and why. Not even collective amnesia can erase the images, for the simple reason that they affected too many people too deeply. The images remain just as vivid today as they were five or ten or fifteen years ago – the Buddhist monk reeling in flames in downtown Saigon, the little Vietnamese girl screaming down the road in pain from her napalmed skin, the man suspected of being Viet Cong grimacing as the executioner's bullet exits from his brain, the bodies at My Lai thrown together in the ditch, the last helicopters leaving Saigon and the masses struggling to get aboard. Saul Maloff writes of these "ineradicable" images that "they present themselves to us as irreducible truth; they are inescapable; they strike us with the force of art; they are not moments among others in a stream of time – they are self-isolating and consummating, burned permanently into the memory traces, absorbing into themselves essential human meaning inviolable by official euphemism and lies."[14]

To render the "essential human meaning" of the Vietnam War has become the intention of many writers and filmmakers. In the past fifteen years Vietnam has been the event most important to literary consciousness in the United States. The number of literary portraits of the war has grown each year since 1965, when Robin Moore's *The Green Berets* became the first American novel written about the Vietnam conflict. Since then, forty to fifty Vietnam novels have been published, though most have been relatively unpopular and unheralded. Only two novels, Robert Stone's *Dog Soldiers* and Tim O'Brien's *Going After Cacciato*, have won National Book Awards and some measure of critical acclaim. Other novels have not been so fortunate, even novels as fine as David Halberstam's *One Very Hot Day*, Victor Kolpacoff's *The Prisoners of Quai Dong*, and Charles Durden's *No Bugles, No Drums*. Nonfiction accounts of the war have had more popular success. Personal narratives such as Michael Herr's *Dispatches*, Philip Caputo's *A Rumor of War*, and Ron Kovic's *Born on the Fourth of July* have been especially praised.

Other books, combining both journalism and history, have been widely read and written about, including C.D.B. Bryan's *Friendly Fire* and Gloria Emerson's *Winners and Losers*. And of course Frances Fitzgerald's very important history, *Fire in the Lake: The Vietnamese and the Americans in Vietnam*, won the Pulitzer Prize, the National Book Award, and the Bancroft Prize for History.

Vietnam movies have proliferated almost as fast as the literature. Hollywood first approached the subject of Vietnam in 1958, when Joseph L. Mankiewicz adapted *The Quiet American* to the screen. Since then, nearly thirty narrative as well as many more documentary Vietnam movies have been released, all of them either tangentially or primarily concerned with the war. Most of these movies, especially the documentaries, have remained obscure. However, with the recent success of movies like *Coming Home, The Deer Hunter,* and *Apocalypse Now,* Hollywood has made Vietnam into a major commercial industry. Altogether, the body of literature and cinema to have come out of the war has been enormous.

Not all the Vietnam books and movies have been enlightening, of course. Many have simply obscured the reality of the war: its origins, its reasons, its consequences. For example, Marin argues that the novels seem "encapsulated in American myths," and that "no novelist seems yet to have been willing to confront, directly, the reality of the war, or to have considered it, at least in part, from the Vietnamese point of view." As a result, the novels "seem to be the work of distraught and alienated men who are unable to locate any sort of vision or binding values."[15] Marin finds the films equally flawed, distorting the war as much as, if not more than, the novels.

Though one can partially agree with Marin's assessment, there are exceptions to his blanket condemnation, as I hope to point out. The next chapter begins with a discussion of Graham Greene's *The Quiet American* for two reasons: it provides a model for later literary responses to the war and it foreshadows how American officials came to misrepresent the war. In Chapter 3 I document this misrepresentation, and in Chapters 4 and 5 I show how official distortions were mirrored in both the broadcast media and literary portraits of the war. Chapter 6 defines and explicates the "dope and dementia" theory as one particular form of literary evasion, especially as found in Michael Herr's *Dispatches.* Later chapters discuss the novels and personal narratives that in one way or another attempt to correct distortions and to clarify important historical, moral, and political questions. Specifically, I argue in Chapter 7 that David Halberstam's *One Very Hot Day* and Tim O'Brien's *Going After Cacciato* resurrect the "secret" history of the war, in Chapter 8 that Victor Kolpacoff's *The Prisoners of Quai Dong* and Robert Stone's *Dog*

Soldiers illuminate the moral dilemmas created by the war, and in Chapter 9 that·Ron Kovic's *Born on the Fourth of July* and Charles Durden's *No Bugles, No Drums* reveal the imperialist aspects of the war. Then, in Chapter 10, the Vietnam movies are discussed—those that derealize Vietnam beyond recognition, and those like *Apocalypse Now* and *Hearts and Minds* that provide important insights into the complexities of the war. The Conclusion points out common trends and elements in what is, considered in its entirety, an extremely dark body of literature and film.

One thing needs to be clear from the beginning: I am not concerned with a purely formalistic analysis here; rather I am interested in this body of literature and film for what it tells us about ourselves and our culture. For these works reflect the difficulties we have in comprehending the war: our evasions, our distortions, our denials. And yet, at the same time, they reflect our limited successes, too. The best of the Vietnam books and films provide an invaluable record of the initial steps we have taken toward facing the unpleasant truth of an unpleasant war.

Chapter 2. A First Warning

The Quiet American

> *Maybe it was already over for us in Indochina when Alden Pyle's body washed up under the bridge at Dakao, his lungs all full of mud; maybe it caved in with Dien Bien Phu.* —Michael Herr, *Dispatches.*

In 1956, in Saigon, that "hot city of yellow and green," Gloria Emerson read the newly-published American edition of *The Quiet American*. Years later, in *Winners and Losers*, she remembered her reaction to Graham Greene's novel: "it was a first warning for me, but I dismissed the book as brilliant but cynical, until it came back to haunt me more than I ever thought such a small, light book ever could."[1] Like Emerson, most

of the growing American community in Saigon dismissed the controversial novel as "anti-American." And of course the novel was anti-
American, in that Greene presented an unsympathetic portrait of United
States intervention in Vietnam, hinting at the tragic outcome of that intervention. In fact, as Emerson wrote in a 1978 interview with Greene, "he
had always understood what was going to happen there, and in that
small quiet novel, told us nearly everything."[2]

As the first, and probably the best, novel to have been written about
the Vietnam War, *The Quiet American* has become a kind of standard in
the eyes of many critics. Zalin Grant, for example, states unequivocally
that "there has been no real challenger to Graham Greene's aging novel."[3]
And Gordon O. Taylor argues that the novel "has become an established
point of reference for those interested in problems of literary response to
the war."[4] Taylor and others consider the novel in some sense "definitive"
of American experience in Vietnam, which speaks well for Greene's success at not only recording but illuminating history. Not that Greene intended to write history; he didn't, as he makes clear in his preface. But he
did write a novel that incorporates historical materials, based on his own
experience as a foreign correspondent in Saigon in the early 1950s. *The
Quiet American* grew out of his own observations of that crucial period
in Vietnamese history when one colonial power replaced another — when
the French-Indochina War became the American-Indochina War.

Greene tells the story of the coming of the Americans to Vietnam
through the eyes of his narrator, Thomas Fowler. A cynical, uncommitted man who prides himself on not having any politics, Fowler works
as an English correspondent and shares his Saigon apartment with a
young Vietnamese woman by the name of Phuong. When not working,
Fowler spends his time smoking opium, drinking at the Continental
Hotel, or enjoying the carnality of his obedient mistress. However, all
that changes when Alden Pyle arrives in Saigon, sent by the State department of the United States on a "secret" mission. No one knows just what
his covert activities involve, only that supposedly he works for the
"Economic Aid Mission." Only later in the novel does Fowler learn the
exact nature of Pyle's "secret" mission, and that knowledge forces him out
of his cynicism and his apathy, forces him to choose sides and to take action against Pyle. *The Quiet American* becomes the story of Fowler's en-
trance into the world of politics and history.

Though 32, the quiet American looks to Fowler as though he had
just walked out of some campus lecture hall. Serious and extremely self-
righteous, with his crew cut and his "wide campus gaze," Pyle seems "incapable of harm." But appearances prove deceptive, and Pyle's innocence
proves anything but harmless, as Fowler soon discovers. At first Fowler's
instincts tell him to protect Pyle, but then he learns "that there was

greater need to protect myself. Innocence always calls mutely for protection, when we would be so much wiser to guard ourselves against it; innocence is like a dumb leper who has lost his bell, wandering the world, meaning no harm."⁵ "God save us always," Fowler remarks, "from the innocent and the good" (p.15).

Pyle comes to Saigon determined to do "good" — "not to any individual person, but to a country, a continent, a world" (p.13). To fill the rapidly evolving power vacuum in Indochina, brought about by the imminent defeat of the French, Pyle and his American colleagues want to build a "national democracy" in South Vietnam. They believe, mistakenly as it turns out, that they can simply create this "national democracy" by the force of their will, their money, and their power. None of them understand that the Vietnamese people are uninterested, concerned only with their land and their way of life. Pyle reveals just how the Americans hope to create this "national democracy" when he lectures Fowler on the necessity of establishing a "third force" in the political arena of South Vietnam, an alternative to the French and the communists. He and the other quiet Americans find their third force in the person of General Thé, a corrupt dissident general holed up on a mountain with his private army. Pyle's secret mission, so Fowler learns, involves his various schemes to build General Thé, a bandit with a few thousand men, into a viable "third force."

In spite of the fact that Fowler regards Pyle's political mission as ludicrous, the two men eventually become friends. Even after Pyle makes off with Fowler's mistress, promising to marry her and take her back to America, to give her children and "respectability," Fowler can ask "am I the only one who really cared for Pyle?" (p.19). And Fowler attempts, throughout the novel, to reveal to Pyle his own naiveté, his silliness in assuming that he can foist "national democracy" off on a people who want the Americans no more than they wanted the French. Pyle has learned nothing about the world except what he has read in books and heard in lecture halls, and he has come to Saigon armed only with academic abstractions. Fowler repeatedly chastises the quiet American for believing that he can shape the world according to his own "romantic" ideas, and for being so self-righteous about his right to shape the world. But Fowler's attitude never becomes simple condemnation, for he feels sorry for Pyle when he notices "that look of pain and disappointment touch his eyes and mouth, when reality didn't match the romantic ideas he cherished" (p.92).

Fowler quickly discovers the source of Pyle's ideas: a writer-diplomat by the name of York Harding. Harding's books include *The Advance of Red China*, *The Role of the West*, and *The Challenge to Democracy*. Pyle speaks of Harding as "York" and carries his copies of the books all the way to Saigon, and it is Harding's "global strategy" that Pyle has been sent to Vietnam to implement. Harding, of course, serves as an obvious parody of John Foster Dulles, secretary of state in the Eisenhower administration from 1953 to 1959 and one of the major architects of the cold war and United States intervention in Southeast Asia. Pyle and the other Americans have all accepted Harding's elucidation of the "domino theory" and the need for the United States to create SEATO organizations and to sow "national democracy" around the world as if it were a rice paddy, there for the planting. Harding's plans, and his global strategy, have deeply affected Pyle, so much so that he has come to see Harding as "almost infallible." "Perhaps I should have seen that fanatic gleam," says Fowler, listening to Pyle praise Harding, "the quick response to a phrase, the magic sound of figures: Fifth Column, Third Force, Seventh Day" (p.23). The Americans fail to see that all the phrases and all the figures exist only in their minds. Harding, as Fowler explains after Pyle's death, "gets hold of an idea and then alters every situation to fit the idea" (p.220). Pyle, too, "got mixed up" (p.220), Fowler concludes, and no one could save him from his borrowed ideas.

The conflict between Fowler and Pyle becomes clearer in a brilliant scene at the center of the novel. Returning from a Coadaist festival, their automobile runs out of gas and the two men find themselves stranded on a deserted highway at dusk. By day the highway tentatively belongs to the French, but by night the highway and the entire countryside belong to the Viet Minh. Along the highway the French have built watchtowers every few hundred yards, and the two of them walk to the nearest tower and prepare to spend the night with two young, frightened Vietnamese soldiers. Fowler pities the young soldiers, employed by the French to sit in the tower night after night waiting for the Viet Minh to creep up through the rice paddies and slit their throats. "Do you think they know they are fighting for democracy?" Fowler asks sarcastically. "We ought to have York Harding here to explain it to them" (p.118). Pyle accuses Fowler of always laughing at "York," and Fowler replies that he laughs at anyone who writes constantly about what does not exist, about "mental concepts" (p.118).

Horrified, Pyle asks Fowler how he can go on living without a belief in something. Fowler's response points to the essential difference between the two men: "...oh, I'm not a Berkeleian. I believe my back's against this wall. I believe there's a sten gun over there.... I even believe what I report" (p.118). Unlike Pyle, Fowler believes in his own experience, in the observable phenomena of external reality as he experiences them and not as they fit into some abstract scheme — in other words he does not look at the world from the point of view of a particular ideology. The Vietnamese do not believe in ideology either, Fowler argues; they simply aren't interested in the war the Americans are trying to sell them, or in the struggle between communism and capitalism. "They want enough rice," Fowler says. "They don't want to be shot at. They want one day to be much the same as another. They don't want our white skins around telling them what they want" (p.119). Pyle's response, straight out of York Harding (John Foster Dulles), typifies all the quiet Americans in the early 1950s: "if Indochina goes –" (p.119). But what does "go" mean? Fowler asks, wagering that in five hundred years New York and London might not exist, but the Vietnamese people will still be growing rice in their paddies. "Isms and ocracies. Give me facts" (p.120), Fowler says, but Pyle has no facts to give, only mental concepts and grandiose global strategies.

Their conversation comes to an abrupt end when the Viet Minh attack the tower. As they flee, Pyle turns to Fowler and asks if he should shoot the two Vietnamese soldiers because he suspects they "were going to hand us over." The "shocking directness" of his question gives Fowler an insight into Pyle's utter insensitivity to human life, an insensitivity that becomes even more apparent later. For when they return to Saigon, Fowler discovers through a network of underground sources just how Pyle intends to implement his plans to bring "national democracy" to South Vietnam. Pyle has been smuggling plastic into the country and supplying General Thé and his bandits with the material to make bombs. In his scheme to build a third force, Pyle even goes so far as to organize a terrorist bombing in downtown Saigon in order to discredit the communists (who will be blamed) and to illustrate the necessity of a strongman dictator, namely General Thé. Pyle's well-laid plans turn out even more dramatically effective than he hoped when a military parade scheduled for the day of the bombing does not take place, and instead of soldiers the bomb kills innocent women and children. Thus Pyle's "national democracy" is born – and dies – in a Saigon bloodbath.

In part, Pyle's problem is perceptual: to him the world and other human lives are raw material to be manipulated according to his abstractions. But even more importantly, his arrogance and his insensitivity to human life lead him to use any means of political power at his disposal, including violence, to create his own reality. Pyle's failure, and the failure of all the quiet Americans, results finally from the absence of moral vision – the failure to imaginatively and sympathetically identify with others. As Fowler realizes, Pyle proves "incapable of conceiving the pain he might cause others" (p.74). And Fowler comes face to face with the enormity of that pain when he witnesses the aftermath of the bombing in downtown Saigon. He stumbles into the Place Garnier, where "a man without legs lay twitching at the edge of the ornamental gardens" (p.214). The sacrifices, Fowler learns, are all paid by others.

Not even the carnage caused by the explosion, however, can jolt the implacable Pyle from his insensitivity. He simply will not acknowledge his own responsibility for the suffering he causes. He makes a feeble attempt to blame the bombing on the communists, but he cannot even convince himself of his own fabrication. Later he comes up with the ultimate rationalization: "they were only war casualties.... It was a pity, but you can't always hit your target. Anyway, they died in the right cause" (p.236). And the right cause just happens to be his cause, of course: "in a way you could say they died for democracy" (p.237). At this point Fowler gives up his attempts to reason with Pyle, for he understands finally that Pyle is "impregnably armored" with his good intentions and his ignorance. "Innocence is a kind of insanity" (p.216), Fowler realizes – a disease.

Earlier a French pilot by the name of Tourin had told Fowler that "we all get involved in a moment of emotion, and then we cannot get out" (pp.200-1). Tourin's words come back to haunt Fowler in the Place Garnier, and he can no longer remain uncommitted. As he watches the man with no legs twitch and the woman hold her dead baby, he decides to commit himself. He knows, as Pyle does not, that a two hundred pound bomb does not discriminate between soldiers and civilians. "How many dead colonels justify a child's or a trishaw driver's death when you are building a national democratic front?" (p.216) he asks, though he already knows the answer: none. He understands that Pyle and the other Americans must be stopped, and he goes directly to the Viet Minh and "sets up" Pyle. And the next day Pyle's body washes up under the bridge at Dakow, his throat slit with a rusty bayonet and his lungs symbolically full of Dakow mud.

Fowler has chosen to enter the complex realm of politics. As he says, "I had become as engagé as Pyle, and it seemed to me that no decision would ever be simple again" (p.242). However, it should not be forgotten that Fowler's decision is based on a moral vision; when he acts, he acts to reaffirm a moral order based on the integrity of human life. In contrast, Pyle's actions throughout the novel reaffirm nothing but a particularly American brand of jingoism, composed of clichés such as "national democracy" that prove contagious to little minds. Pyle has no values but platitudes, no morality but abstractions and strategies. Unlike Pyle, who learns nothing from his experience in Vietnam, Fowler finally acts because he comes to understand that "sooner or later ... one has to take sides – if one is to remain human" (p.230). Gordon O. Taylor stresses the importance of Fowler's moral vision in arguing that "the true terrain of *The Quiet American*, beyond the historical and cartographical accuracy of its setting, is the moral ground on which Fowler eventually takes sides in order to remain human."[6]

Even more importantly, Fowler's decision to become engaged, and therefore to deal himself into history, can be seen as the fictional equivalent of Graham Greene's own decision as a writer to take the material for his fiction out of history itself. Fowler chooses to take sides against the Americans, and Greene chooses to write an indictment of American involvement in Vietnam, for the same political and moral reasons: the act of writing mirrors the fiction itself. Greene's "historical and cartographical accuracy" constitutes an attempt to interpret, possibly even to change, history. Though his novel could not expel any of the very real quiet Americans descending on Saigon in the 1950s, the novel attempts to influence history in a less direct way—by arousing world opinion against American involvement in Vietnam. Greene also takes sides; his commitment to history provides *The Quiet American* with its very powerful critical perspective.

The Quiet American offers important insights into the future course of the war, for the character of Alden Pyle anticipates military and State department officials who attempted just as blatantly to create the ever-elusive "third force." Greene also anticipates the surreality of the war, which partly resulted from official misrepresentation of what was happening in Vietnam, from the disparity between reality itself and the official version of it. Just as Pyle imprisons himself in his own abstractions, American officials were never able to free themselves from their own propaganda, so that the war came to seem an insane abyss. American officials "spoke in words that had no currency left as words, sentences with no hope of meaning in the sane world," Michael Herr writes in *Dispatches*,[7] referring specifically to their progress reports and their victory speeches. Pyle spoke these words too. Greene's prophetic account of the beginning of the second Indochina war remains unequalled among the literature of the Vietnam War.

Graham Greene's achievement in *The Quiet American* provoked some angry responses in America. The novel was too explicitly political for American audiences, too "cynical." Reviewing the book in *The New Yorker*, A.J. Leibling attacked it as a "nasty little plastic bomb." Leibling went on to argue that there was a difference "between calling your over-successful ally a silly ass and accusing him of murder."[8] Today, the distinction between a silly ass and a murderer has become rather blurred. Perhaps we are all quiet Americans.

Chapter 3. Official Distortions 1950-1975

"No Exit onto Reality"

> *The dialogue of Saigon turned around on its own axis, giving no exit onto reality.* — Frances Fitzgerald, *Fire in the Lake.*

The Quiet American angered many of the Americans living in Saigon in 1956. They did not want to acknowledge the possibility that American intervention in Southeast Asia could fail. Americans did not fail. Given the necessary investment of money and power, success would be assured. They believed that social and historical reality could be constructed like a house of cards, that Vietnam could be reshaped to fit their press releases. Moreover, the Americans did not want to be associated with the French, for that was history and history did not matter. Gloria Emerson recalls that "among us, in Saigon, there was not much interest in the French; the Americans learned nothing from them. All that mattered was that the French had failed, not the reasons why."[1] Anyway, the Americans saw themselves not as imperialists but anticommunists, wanting only to keep Vietnam free from the worldwide communist conspiracy. According to Emerson, "all of us were not unlike Pyle: earnest, ignorant, friendly, hygienic, preachy. We talked the way he did. 'If Vietnam goes...' became an obsession, a blue-eyed marching song"[2] that led America into an undeclared war that lasted nineteen more years.

Though fiction, *The Quiet American* correctly reveals how the Americans came to be involved in Vietnam. By 1954 the Eisenhower administration, and leading politicians from both parties, had come to regard Vietnam as vital to American interests in Asia. They felt threatened by the victory of the Chinese revolution led by Mao Tse-Tung, and they had decided upon a policy of "containment" as articulated by John Foster Dulles and Dean Acheson before him. With the United Nations police action in Korea and continued support for Chiang Kai-Shek, they attempted to build a wall of anticommunist enclaves dependent upon the United States. Vietnam constituted the crucial southern part of the wall, according to their strategy. Consequently, in 1950 the Truman administration began to subsidize the French war in Vietnam, and by 1954 the United States was paying for nearly 80 percent of all French military expenditures in Vietnam. In fact, President Eisenhower considered committing tactical nuclear weapons or American air power to prop up the failing French effort. During the siege of Dien Bien Phu, Eisenhower had the Joint Chiefs of Staff compose a contingency plan for an air strike on the attacking Viet Minh, but the raid never materialized because Eisenhower could not win the support of key congressional leaders or of his allies (Eisenhower insisted that England and at least one or two Asian nations be a part of such a "joint act"). Even after the fall of Dien Bien Phu, the United States government did everything possible to "cajole the French to stay in the fight as long as possible," in the words of Bernard Fall.[3]

The enthusiasm for this crusade against communism can be partly explained by the fact that the early 1950s was the height of the McCarthy era. In Washington the senator from Wisconsin had attacked certain State department officials who recommended that the United States recognize Mao Tse-Tung's victory in China. Senator McCarthy called them "traitors" and saw their like and others he thought were communists everywhere, even inside the American government, conspiring with the Kremlin. Unfortunately, leading public officials from both parties were only too willing to borrow McCarthy's rhetoric, accutely aware of the political benefits of such a hardline stand. For example, Vice President Nixon charged the Democrats with the "loss of China" and "softness" on communism. Later, Senator John F. Kennedy appropriated the domino theory from the Truman and Eisenhower administrations. Kennedy and Senator Mike Mansfield became charter members of a group that called itself American Friends of Vietnam, a group that supported "independence" for the State of Vietnam, which translated into support for the state of South Vietnam created and organized by the French. At a meeting of American Friends of Vietnam in 1956, Kennedy referred to Vietnam as "the cornerstone of the Free World in Southeast Asia." If Vietnam "fell," he insisted, then "Burma, Thailand, India, Japan, the Philippines, and obviously Laos and Cambodia" would be swept away by the "red tide."[4]

This fear of those who called themselves communists, and the foreign policy that grew out of it, acted as blinders that prevented the American government from seeing the political realities of Vietnam. A good example of the conclusions that this blindness encouraged was Nixon's statement on December 27, 1953, that "if China were not Communist, there would be no war in Indochina,"[5] a statement that demonstrated complete ignorance of the Vietnam conflict. The Vietnamese people had been struggling for decades against the French colonialists, intensely so since 1945 when the French Army reoccupied Vietnam at the end of World War II — four full years before the establishment of the People's Republic of China. The conceit that Ho Chi Minh was a "puppet" of Moscow has been discredited once and for all by Archimedes Patti's recent book, *Why Viet Nam?* (1980). Patti headed a United States oss delegation to Indochina in 1945, and he had extensive dealings with Ho Chi Minh, who worked closely with the Americans on a number of clandestine missions against the Japanese. In fact, when Ho Chi Minh organized the Democratic Republic of Vietnam (DRVN) in August of 1945, Viet Minh guerrillas, armed and trained and supported by oss agents, were fighting the Japanese only forty miles from Hanoi. Patti carefully documents the fact that Ho Chi Minh was a nationalist first, and a communist second. Ho Chi Minh made repeated appeals to Patti, and to other oss and State department officials, for assistance in the face of an imminent French return to Vietnam. As the surviving documents make clear, the Vietnamese leader considered the United States the only possible source of support for an independent Vietnam. After World War II, Russia was too weakened by its war effort to provide much assistance, and China under Chiang Kai-Shek was overtly hostile to the Vietnamese, as it had been for centuries. (The Soviet Union and China recognized the DRVN only in 1950, five years after the beginning of the Viet Minh's guerrilla war against the French.) Even more to the point, Ho Chi Minh considered the United States the "champion of freedom." Though capitalist, the United States stood alone among the Western powers in not having a history of colonialism.

However, Ho Chi Minh's overtures to the United States fell on deaf ears, for at the time American officials did not want to disrupt Franco-American affairs. Later, the United States refused support because the Vietnamese leader was seen as a communist puppet. Dean Acheson went so far as to refer to him as "the mortal enemy of native independence in Indochina."[6] But the fact remains, as Patti argues, that "only Ho Chi Minh had for over a quarter of a century kept the torch for independence burning in the hearts and minds of the Vietnamese, both Communist and nonCommunist, that he alone had become the personification of Vietnamese nationalism."[7] The blindness of the Americans, the missed chance to live up to Ho Chi Minh's image of America as the champion of freedom, leads Patti to conclude that these early events in Vietnam constitute the "saddest episode in American history."[8]

But the fear of communism only partly explains the willingness of the American government to intervene in Vietnam on the side of the French. Also important was the inherited colonialist assumption that the Vietnamese people, being somehow inferior to their Western protectors, could not govern themselves. Many government documents, published in *The Pentagon Papers* and Gareth Porter's *Vietnam: A History in Documents*, reveal the pervasiveness of the assumption that "the Vietnamese were incapable of governing themselves, and that only a steadying European [or American] hand would prevent anarchy, followed by the extinction of all freedom."[9] In fact, the first State department draft memorandum on policy toward post war Indochina argued that the Vietnamese would "require further preparation of unspecified duration before being allowed to govern themselves."[10] A 1947 telegram from George C. Marshall to the French government asserted that the Vietnamese required "enlightened political guidance," a guidance that could only come from a nation "steeped like France in democratic tradition."[11] These arguments look forward to later, racist statements by American generals and politicians concerning the "oriental mind." General Westmoreland took this attitude to its logical conclusion in his well-known public remark that Orientals do not place the same value on human life that "we" do, that to them human life is not "important."

The rhetoric might have remained only rhetoric but for one unfortunate turn of history: the French lost. Suddenly the United States could no longer fight communism by proxy in Vietnam. When the French garrison at Dien Bien Phu fell to the Viet Minh on May 7, 1954, the French could no longer continue the war. However, instead of simply withdrawing from Vietnam, the French persuaded the DRVN to negotiate the entire question of Indochina at an international conference that included France, England, the Soviet Union, the People's Republic of China, and the United States. The Geneva Conference began consideration of the

Indochina problem on May 8, 1954, and in the next two months the conference issued two separate documents, an Armistice and a Final Declaration. The Armistice, signed by the French and the DRVN, provided for an exchange of prisoners and withdrawal of both armies to either side of the 17th parallel. The Final Declaration, in Frances Fitzgerald's summary, "specified that the demilitarized zone should not constitute a political or territorial boundary, but merely a temporary military demarcation line. Following the period of truce, a political settlement should be made on the basic of 'respect for the principles of independence, unity, and territorial integrity' of Vietnam and by means of free general elections to be held in July 1956."[12] Neither of the documents made any reference to a second state in Vietnam; each side was to administer its regroupment zone during the period of armistice. Reunification was to occur in July of 1956.

None of the participants in the Geneva Conference ever signed the Final Declaration because the United States "refused even to give its oral consent," Fitzgerald argues in *Fire in the Lake*.[13] For whatever reason, the document was not signed (though it was agreed to by voice vote, an "unsigned treaty" that many historians, including Archimedes Patti, consider legally binding under international law). President Eisenhower revealed his attitude toward the political settlement in a June 30 press conference when he spoke of "peace with honor" and "coexistence without appeasement," adding that the United States would not be "a party to any agreement that makes anybody a slave." That line, according to Bernard Fall, demonstrated a "clear cut dissociation of the United States from the cease-fire negotiations."[14] Not only did the United States refuse to accept the prospect of an eventual reunification of Vietnam under the DRVN, it would not accept the already accomplished DRVN control above the 17th parallel. As Fitzgerald records, American officials had ambitions "not only to build up a government in Saigon, but to undermine Ho Chi Minh's government as well."[15] To accomplish this, the Eisenhower administration sent a variety of officials to Saigon, representing secret agencies. The efforts of one official, Colonel Edward G. Lansdale, bear unmistakable resemblance to Alden Pyle's "secret" mission in *The Quiet American*. In June Lansdale was sent to Vietnam as head of a Saigon military mission with orders to "beat the Geneva timetable of Communist takeover in the north." By August, Lansdale's teams were scattered across North Vietnam conducting sabotage operations in direct violation of the United States government's promise to avoid violence during the period of negotiated truce. (Though the United States would not sign the Final Declaration, Walter Bedell Smith issued an official declaration to the Geneva Conference on July 21, 1954, to the effect that the United States would "refrain from the threat or the use of force to disturb" the agreements of the conference.[16]) Years later *The Pentagon Papers* and *Vietnam: A History in Documents* made public some of Lansdale's activities, which included terrorist acts, referred to as "black psywar strikes" in official jargon, such as "contaminating the oil supply of the bus company [in Hanoi] for a gradual wreckage of engines in the buses" and "taking the first actions for delayed sabotage of the railroad," as their own reports would have it.[17] Like Pyle's in *The Quiet American,* Lansdale's mission was to discredit the communists and to create a third force in the political arena of South Vietnam.

Two months after the Geneva Conference ended, John Foster Dulles created the Southeast Asia Treaty Organization (SEATO), an organization of states that agreed to assist each other against armed aggression from the outside. At first the treaty included only three Asian nations — Thailand, Pakistan, and the Philippines — but a separate protocol covered Cambodia, Laos, and the "State of Vietnam." Now all the United States needed was a government to assist and it could, under the pretense of international law, continue the war. This presented a problem, because governments were scarce in Saigon in 1954. After their defeat, the French left South Vietnam under the imaginary rule of Bao Dai, chief of state of the "State of Vietnam." Bao Dai, however, had spent the last four years big-game hunting in the resort city of Dalat, for the simple reason that he had nothing to do in Saigon since the French effectively controlled all affairs of state. Even when the French military effort collapsed at Dien Bien Phu, Bao Dai declined to assert his claim as the legitimate government of South Vietnam. Instead, while the Geneva Conference was deliberating, Bao Dai fled to France and in effect abdicated to his prime minister, Ngo Dinh Diem.

As it turned out, Bao Dai was no fool. South Vietnam had become, in Fitzgerald's words, a "political jungle of war lords, sects, bandits, partisan troops, and secret societies."[18] Bernard Fall lived in Saigon in 1954, and he described these bandit generals and politicians and their "slide into unreality": "various Vietnamese politicians (none representing anything more than a few close friends and family members) were making grandiloquent statements on how they would continue to fight on 'to total victory,' and hatching far-reaching schemes for this end."[19] This political jungle turned out to be Diem's legacy, which he inherited by default from Bao Dai, who refused to risk his life in an attempt to consolidate a nonexistent government. Like Bao Dai, Diem had been in exile for four years, though Diem had been hunting bigger game than that found at Dalat. In 1950 Diem came to America, where he became friends with several influential public figures, among them John F. Kennedy. A Catholic, Diem was received enthusiastically by Francis Cardinal Spellman and other leading representatives of the Catholic church. Diem even lived for two years at the Maryknoll seminaries in New Jersey and New York and lectured occasionally in American universities. When he returned to Vietnam in June of 1954, Diem had influential American contacts who would support his cause — and that eventually proved more important than the lack of public support he found in Saigon, among his own countrymen. And when, shortly after Diem's return, Colonel Edward Lansdale paid a visit to Diem in the palace of the former governor general, the Americans had, like Alden Pyle in *The Quiet American*, found their man.

The Americans wanted to throw their support behind the strongest possible candidate, the man who stood the best chance of bringing order to the political chaos of Saigon. More than any other individual, Colonel Edward Lansdale was responsible for convincing Washington that Diem would, with appropriate American backing, become their "third force." Lansdale went to work for Diem, actually going to live in the palace and becoming what Fitzgerald refers to as a "two-way agent": "on the one hand, Diem's personal contact man and adviser in the attempt to win over the diverse political elements of the South, and on the other an advocate for Diem within the American mission."[20] Though as late as April 1955, Secretary of State Dulles was considering a "replacement" for Diem, Lansdale's advocacy proved decisive. The Americans wasted no time, as President Eisenhower pledged direct economic aid and military assistance in a letter to Diem on October 24, 1954; and the United States began to train and reorganize Diem's army in February of 1955. With American support, Diem moved quickly to consolidate his power. He began to dissociate himself from Bao Dai, who was still the titular emperor of the "State of Vietnam," and in April 1955 his army successfully attacked the private army of the Binh Xuyen, a rival political faction that had controlled both organized crime and the national police under Bao Dai. In July Diem repudiated the Geneva accords, specifically the article providing for free elections to unite the two parts of Vietnam. Instead, Diem organized a referendum to determine whether South Vietnam should be a monarchy under Bao Dai or a republic with himself as president. The referendum took place in October of 1955, and Diem received 99 percent of the vote (including 605,025 votes from the total of 450,000 registered voters in Saigon).

For the moment, however, the Americans had their third force. The Americans paid the bill for Diem's government, and they trained and equipped the army that kept Diem in power. But the social engineering of the Americans went far beyond this, for in 1955 a team from Michigan State University, consisting of some fifty scholars and public administrators and headed by Dr. Wesley Fishel, went to Vietnam to reorganize the Diem administration, the police, and the civil guard. The

Americans — their politicians, their generals, and their social scientists — created the entire edifice. As in a magic show, something out of nothing. The problem proved to be reality, which kept encroaching on the Diem illusion until it finally burst in a back street of Saigon.

Nevertheless, the State department soon began to praise Diem as an able leader who was on the way to rebuilding the economy and solving the social problems of South Vietnam. With the rhetoric of their own public relations campaign, they packaged Diem for the press and the United States Congress. To the discredit of the press, it accepted the official line almost without question, printing and verifying the propaganda pumped out daily at State department briefings. The press hailed Diem as a man of "deep religious heart" who, according to *Life*, had "saved his people from [the] agonizing prospect" of national elections; this "tough miracle man" had built a nation in South Vietnam and halted "the red tide of Communism in Asia." The *Saturday Evening Post* called South Vietnam "the Bright Spot in Asia," proclaiming "two years ago at Geneva, South Vietnam was virtually sold down the river to the Communists. Today the spunky little Asian country is back on its own feet, thanks to a 'mandarin in a sharkskin suit' who's upsetting the Red timetable."[21] *Newsweek* praised Diem as "one of Asia's ablest leaders," and *Time* called him "doughty little Diem."[22]

Diem was given a hero's welcome when he visited the United States in 1957. President Eisenhower received him at the airport and praised him as the personification of patriotism in his part of the world. Diem addressed a joint session of Congress and visited New York, where Mayor Robert Wagner referred to him as "a man history may yet adjudge as one of the great men of the twentieth century."[23] During his tour of the United States, *The New York Times* complimented Diem for his "firm concept of human rights."[24] By the time President Johnson referred to Diem as "the Winston Churchill of Asia" in 1961, words and reality had long since parted company, never to be rejoined.[25]

How American officials managed to conceal the true nature of the Diem regime remains a mystery. Quite early in his reign, Diem began to impose censorship on the press, closing down newspapers that printed any criticism of his government. Diem jailed political opponents and parcelled out power to members of his family and a few close friends. In 1956 Diem issued an ordinance calling for the arrest and detention of persons considered dangerous to the state, an ordinance that gave him a legal excuse to create political prison camps and to suspend habeas corpus laws. In 1959 he issued yet another law setting up military tribunals to deal with infringements of national security. These tribunals gave no rights to defendants and handed down sentences only of life imprisonment or death. Much of South Vietnam resembled a concentration camp, where only Diem's followers enjoyed human rights, and even then only insofar as they remained in his favor. The "national democracy" that Americans so desired had turned overnight into an absolute dictatorship.

Still, by this time the American propaganda machine ran on its own momentum. American officials ignored the existence of the prison camps and the institutional tyranny of the Diem regime, and they talked repeatedly about Diem's "strong leadership," by which they meant a leadership that had kept South Vietnam out of the hands of the communists. And when they could no longer overlook the fact that Diem was a dictator, they attempted to justify his dictatorship with a sophistry that set the tone for American involvement in Vietnam. For example, in a 1959 article in the *New Leader* entitled "Vietnam's Democratic One-Man Rule," Dr. Wesley Fishel argued that "Ngo Dinh Diem has all the authority and all the power one needs to operate a dictatorship, but he isn't operating one! Here is a leader who speaks the language of democracy, who holds the power of a dictator, who governs a Republic in accordance with the terms of a Constitution." Fishel went on to explain that "the peoples of Southeast Asia are not, generally speaking, sufficiently sophisticated to understand what we mean by democracy and how they can exercise and protect their own political rights"[26]: again the old colonialist assumption about the "Oriental mind" and the benefits of further education at the hands of Westerners. American officials were both blind and duplicitous. They deceived themselves, and their country, then came to believe their own deceptions. The Diem regime had, in Fitzgerald's words, become "a fiction to them, an autonomous creation of the mind."[27]

The fiction had to end, as Diem withdrew further and further from the people, estranged from everyone but his friends and family. When his people finally rose against him, Diem could only respond with further repression. On June 16, 1963, a Buddhist bonze by the name of Thich Quang Duc immolated himself in a busy intersection in downtown Saigon. From that moment on, the days of the Diem regime were numbered. Events finally came to a head in August, when Ngo Dinh Nhu, Diem's powerful brother, ordered his troops to shoot more than 30 Buddhist bonzes a few hundred yards from the palace and then arrested thousands of students who demonstrated against this action. Then Nhu made a fatal mistake—he publicly attacked the United States government and charged that the CIA chief in Saigon (John Richardson) had formed a plot against his life. Having lived by the Americans, Diem and his brother died in a military coup supported by the Americans on November 1, 1963. The brothers were taken to a backstreet in Saigon and shot like thieves.

American complicity in Diem's overthrow is demonstrated in recently published State department documents. The Americans had created Diem, and when he no longer served their purpose, they threw their support to a group of dissident generals plotting a coup. President Kennedy and his top advisers — Ambassador Henry Cabot Lodge, CIA station chief John Richardson, and the commander of the Military Assistance Command Vietnam, General Paul Harkins — negotiated from August 24 to October 30, 1963, the fate of Ngo Dinh Diem. "We must face the possibility that Diem himself cannot be preserved," wrote acting Secretary of State George Ball to Henry Cabot Lodge in a telegram on August 24, as the Americans prepared to take back what they had given. Ball continued: "we are prepared to accept the obvious implication that we can no longer support Diem. You may tell appropriate military commanders we will give them direct support in any interim period of breakdown central government mechanism."[28]

In a telegram from Secretary of State Dean Rusk to Lodge on August 29, Lodge was authorized to establish liaison with potential coup planners and given the authority to announce suspension of aid to Diem at a time of his own choosing. His instructions were to do everything "to minimize appearance of collusion with generals."[29] The power brokering continued until October 31, the day before the actual coup, when McGeorge Bundy cabeled Lodge that "once a coup under responsible leadership has begun ... it is in the interest of the U.S. government that it should succeed."[30] Contact with the generals had been established, plans for the coup had been laid, and the following day Diem and his brother were dead.

After Diem's assassination, the military coup became commonplace in the politics of South Vietnam. The scenario was always the same — dissident generals plotting, jockeying for American support, then scrambling for power as one military government replaced another and history repeated itself endlessly. Most of the governments fell just as quickly as they came to power. General Duong Van Minh, General Nguyen Khanh, General Tran Thien Khiem, General Lam Van Phat, Air Marshal Nguyen Kao Ky, General Nguyen Van Thieu — their governments carbon copies of each other, variations on the Diem theme of corruption and tyranny. None of the governments could establish its own legitimacy; none could win the support of more than a fraction of the South Vietnamese people.

The last of these governments fell on April 30, 1975, as South Vietnamese soldiers fled without resistance before the advancing armies of the DRVN. The entire facade of the South Vietnamese government collapsed in disgrace, as high-ranking officials all scrambled to get out of the country on American ships and planes. President Thieu, resigning on April 21, vowed to stay on and fight: "I resign but I do not desert.... I will continue to stay close to you all in the coming task of national defense."[31]

Five days later Thieu packed 15 tons of "baggage" into a U.S. Air Force C-118 transport plane and flew to Taipei, taking with him three and a half tons of South Vietnamese gold. Former Vice President Ky was not far behind — three days, to be exact. After telling a crowd of Catholics in Saigon to "let the cowards run away with the Americans" and promising to lead a defense of the capital, Ky commandeered a helicopter and flew it to the deck of the *USS Midway* waiting off the coast of Vietnam.[32] T.D. Allman described the fall of the Saigon regime:

> The South Vietnamese soldiers fleeing an enemy which has not yet attacked and trying to push their motor bikes on to U.S. ships sums up the product of American "nation-building" — a militarist society with nothing worth fighting for; a consumer society that produces nothing; a nation of abandoned women conditioned to flee to the next handout of U.S. surplus rice; of dispossessed gangs hitching rides on U.S. planes to the next jerry-built urban slum.[33]

Reality itself caught up with the Americans too on April 30. For over twenty years they had been engaged in a process of social and historical engineering that took them further and further into their own labyrinthine unrealities, compounded year after year by more and more new "programs" — pacification programs, strategic hamlet programs, land reform programs. After years of discussion and news briefings, these programs came to be accepted facts, necessary and immutable; no one questioned their existence, only measured their effectiveness by charts and figures in briefing rooms. Once begun, the process did not lend itself to correction, because there was no critical perspective built into military and State department bureaucracies. American officials found themselves locked in a closed system. "The job of the American ambassador, the military command, the heads of the aid programs, the CIA operations groups, and their counterparts in Washington, was not to discover if the American effort was morally wrong or doomed to failure, but to make that war effort a success," Fitzgerald wrote.[34] Surrealism was institutional.

To demonstrate the success of the war effort, American officials relied on their ability to produce statistics. In the absence of any discernible objective, statistics suggested that the war effort was accomplishing something, that it had produced tangible results. The war became a war of attrition, in which success was measured by the body count — the number of dead Viet Cong and North Vietnamese soldiers. Likewise, the success of the social programs was measured by the number of refugees relocated, the number of strategic hamlets, etc. Numbers and more numbers, until obsession became fetish. "Instead of honesty," C.D.B. Bryan writes in *Friendly Fire*, "Americans were given numbers: body counts, tonnage counts, mission counts, truck counts, troop counts, weapons counts ... counts? ... The word had become alien and meaningless in its repetitions. It was as if the government believed numbers, through their inviolability, could sanctify and shore up [their] policy."[35] But the numbers themselves were not inviolable. The system put enormous pressure on officials to exaggerate or falsify their figures, body counts being only the most widely known of these abuses. Like everything else, the numbers became so many fictions.

When forced out from behind their numbers, American officials engaged in a deliberate policy to deceive. It became the official policy of five different American administrations to "minimize" the American involvement in Vietnam. For example, Kennedy's Assistant Secretary of State Robert Manning articulated "the long-standing desire of the United States government to see the American involvement minimized, even represented as something less in reality than it is."[36] Such deception occurred until the very end of active American participation under the Nixon administration, with its secret invasion of Cambodia and its Christmas bombing of Hanoi. The record of these administrations, as evidenced in the documents published in *The Pentagon Papers*, prompted Bryan to write: "what was so troubling about the Pentagon Papers was not so much the disclosures of deceitful and ill-chosen policies, but the obvious contempt with which one presidential administration after another viewed Congress and the American people."[37]

Instead of news, the war correspondents sent to Saigon to report the war found only euphemisms, half-truths, and outright lies. They were told repeatedly that military victory was in sight, when in fact the Viet Cong and North Vietnamese could and did match the U.S. military build-up step by step, the two sides locked in a deadly spiral with no end in sight. They were told repeatedly that the social programs were winning the hearts and minds of the Vietnamese people, when in fact the strategic hamlets turned out to be little more than concentration camps, and the pacification program a misguided policy that created millions of refugees. In the end, in a nation of nine million refugees clotting the camps and the urban slums waiting for the next handout from the Americans, all talk of social revolution and nation-building "evidenced an extreme removal from reality," Fitzgerald wrote.[38]

Official distortions of reality were so great that Michael Herr, who covered the war for *Esquire* magazine, later wrote that "the spokesmen spoke in words that had no currency left as words, sentences without meaning in the sane world."[39] When their efforts at social and historical engineering began to collapse, American officials worked harder at holding reality and the official version of reality together, producing an intolerable tension that sought release not so much in protest against the United States government as in scorn and resentment against the

Vietnamese. Thus the Americans came to hate them, to regard them as "weak" and "corrupt": not our illusions, but the unworthy Vietnamese had betrayed us down the long and winding road to final defeat.

Like Alden Pyle in *The Quiet American,* the Americans got hold of an idea and altered every situation to fit the idea. They ignored the social, political, and historical background of the Vietnamese people. In a discussion that could have been written about the quiet Americans in Vietnam, Gerald Graff argues that while it is true that our intellect imposes its ideas "upon the inarticulate mass of our 'sensations' and thereby brings order to them," it is also true that "we rarely succeed with our impositions, that we try and err again and again, and that the result — our knowledge of the world — owes as much to the resisting reality as to our self-produced ideas."[40] This knowledge of the world has eluded us in Vietnam; not only did we mistakenly attempt to construct our own version of Vietnamese reality, our culture has failed to learn the lessons of our encounter with the resisting reality of Vietnam.

The result, of course, has been cultural confusion. After living so long with the distortions of official propaganda, our belief in the possibility of determining what really happened in Vietnam has been eroded. Nowhere does this confusion become more apparent than in some of the literature and films that have come out of the war. At their worst, these creative efforts repeat official distortions of the war, failing to illuminate how the war came to be wrapped in the myth that it was incomprehensible. At best, these efforts present the reality of the war and demonstrate that "a sense of unreality is not a legal defense" (a point made by one of the characters in Robert Stone's *Dog Soldiers*).[41] As a character in Charles Durden's *No Bugles, No Drums* realizes, "reality has a way of snatchin' right back. You don't fuck reality around too much."[42] Such is the lesson of Vietnam.

Chapter 4. Media Distortions

"History's Heavy Attrition"

> *Conventional journalism could no more reveal this war than conventional firepower could win it, all it could do was take the most profound event of the American decade and turn it into a communications pudding, taking its most obvious, undeniable history and making it into a secret history.* — Michael Herr, *Dispatches*.

The American news media by and large contributed to and legitimized official distortions of the Vietnam War. The military command in Saigon, the administration in Washington, and the news media all fed into the same closed circuit. The military told Washington what it wanted to hear, and the press made certain that all the progress reports and all the victory speeches got coverage. "It was inevitable," Michael Herr argues in *Dispatches*, "that once the media took the diversions seriously enough to report them, they also legitimized them."¹ Given the interconnection of these institutions, legitimacy was conferred automatically.

By printing and televising official misrepresentations of the war, the news media magnified them. The media overlooked obvious parallels between the French and American Indochinese wars and failed to expose how the United States had come to be involved in the war, first backing the French in 1950 and then the Diem regime in 1954, as if one day the war had simply appeared on the network news, had sprung full-blown onto the front page of *The New York Times*. "History's heavy attrition," Herr calls it: "For all the books and articles and white papers, all the talk and the miles of film, something wasn't answered, it wasn't even asked.... [T]here was a secret history, and not a lot of people felt like running in there to bring it out," Herr remarks.²

To its discredit, the news media did not reveal the American government's attempt to recreate Vietnam, laying siege to that small distant nation "in pursuit of a pretty, tantalizing, promiscuous, particularly American brand of government," Tim O'Brien writes in *If I Die in a Combat Zone*.³ Two thousand years of Vietnamese history, a civilization many times older than ours, went virtually unnoticed by the media. During twenty years of war, only Bernard Fall and Frances Fitzgerald published serious studies of the culture and history of the Vietnamese people. More importantly, the media failed to challenge the government's attitude toward history — the belief that history can be created like a commodity. This point needs further clarification, because it partially explains the arrogance of the Americans toward the Vietnamese. The Americans were not simply ahistorical; they believed that history could be created or erased whenever it served their purposes. This view of history follows from the assumption that reality can be shaped according to preconceived ideas or abstractions, "mental concepts" as Graham Greene refers to them in *The Quiet American*. The efforts of the Americans to remake Vietnamese society necessitated a distortion or denial of history, because history pulls at the present, restricting the ways it can be shaped. Only by denying history could the Americans imagine accomplishing their purpose in Vietnam. So deny they did.

Without the critical perspective provided by history, the news media simply passed on official distortions of the war. However, to be fair, the media's failure to make the war intelligible to the American public can partly be explained by its limited access to reliable information. In the early years, from 1954 until 1963, journalists in South Vietnam found themselves under enormous pressure from the Diem

regime to report favorably on the war effort. The journalists were ac-
credited by the Diem government, and if they wrote stories critical of
Diem's performance, "the Diem regime called them spies and Communists, and did its best to censor their copy and, by intimidation,
prevent them from repeating the offense," Phillip Knightley writes in *The
First Casualty*.⁴ Over the years, as Diem withdrew into his own circle of
friends, his efforts at censorship became more blatant. For example,
Diem issued an expulsion order against veteran reporter François Sully
who wrote an article for *Newsweek* on August 22, 1962 entitled "Vietnam: The Unpleasant Truth." Sully wrote that the war was a "losing
proposition" and quoted Bernard Fall as saying that Diem's government
was inadequate. For his efforts, Sully was forced to leave the country, as
was an NBC correspondent who happened to remark that an interview
with Diem was a "waste of time."⁵ One of the first big stories of the war
broke on June 9, 1963, when Thich Quang Duc immolated himself in
downtown Saigon. Forewarned of the event, Junius Browne of the
Associated Press photographed the immolation, and the next day his
photographs and story made front-page news around the world. Diem
reacted swiftly, increasing his intimidation, suspecting all members of the
press, not trusting anyone in the last days of his regime. His secret police,
Knightley writes, "tapped their telephones, monitored their telex
machines, planted agents in their offices, and tried to follow them in the
streets."⁶ When Diem was murdered in a military coup on November 30,
the grisly photographs of his bullet-ridden body were flashed around the
world, courtesy of the news media.

Washington, too, pressured the news media in its own way. The
Kennedy administration did everything possible to supress the full extent
of American involvement in Vietnam, as evidenced by the notorious
Cable 1006 from the State department to its information service in
Saigon. The cable "warned against providing transport for correspondents
producing undesirable stories." Kennedy even asked *New York Times*
publisher "Punch" Sulzberger to reassign David Halberstam, an experienced reporter whom Kennedy considered particularly troublesome. To
his credit, Sulzberger refused to comply, as Halberstam recalls in *The
Making of a Quagmire*. But while officials of the Military Assistance Ad-
visory Group attempted to limit the media's access to information in
Saigon, State department officials attempted to pressure the editors of
influential newspapers and magazines back in the states. In *Dispatches*
Michael Herr remembers the "incredible demands put on [journalists]
from offices thousands of miles away."⁷ The problem, Herr argues,
derived from the fact that the correspondents worked "for organizations
that were ultimately reverential toward the institutions involved: the
Office of the President, the Military," etc.⁸ Thus the corespondents often

found that their stories had been substantially altered by the time their accounts finally reached print. For example, in August, 1963, Charles Mohr and Merton Perry wrote a long evaluation of the war effort at the request of their editors at *Time*. As written, their first sentence read: "The war in Vietnam is being lost." However, this line completely disappeared from the published version, which totally inverted their position and claimed that the war was going well and that "government troops are fighting better than ever."[9] These kinds of "corrections" occurred frequently throughout the war.

After Diem's assassination, official censorship was never as severe, even though as late as 1967 a journalist as famous as Martha Gellhorn could be denied a visa to reenter South Vietnam after writing a series of five articles that criticized United States military strategy in Vietnam. When no newspaper in the United States would accept the series of articles, Gellhorn published them in the *Guardian*, an English newspaper. Her career as a journalist in South Vietnam came to an abrupt end because she acknowledged that "we, unintentionally, are killing and wounding three or four times more people than the Vietcong do, so we are told, on purpose." She went on to say that:

> We are not maniacs and monsters, but our planes range the sky all day and all night, and our artillery is lavish and we have much more deadly stuff to kill with. The people are there on the ground, sometimes destroyed by accident, sometimes destroyed because Vietcong are reported to be among them. This is indeed a new kind of war, as the indoctrination lecture stated, and we had better find a new way to fight it. Hearts and minds, after all, live in bodies.[10]

Instead of censorship, the United States and South Vietnamese governments later attempted to disseminate their version of the war by an extensive public relations campaign. As both sides escalated the war from 1963 on, correspondents found themselves subjected to repeated appeals to their "patriotism" and the "national interest," harangues to "get with the program, jump on the team, come in for the Big Win," to quote Michael Herr.[11] Attending official press conferences, the correspondents were given outright fabrications contradicting what they knew to be true of the ever-widening war. Herr remembers the "mindless optimism" of the military, the "kind that had seen us through Tet, smiling in the shambles ... the kind that rejected facts and killed grunts wholesale and drove you into mad, helpless rage."[12] Herr's point needs to be emphasized, because too often the consequences of such "mindless optimism" are not acknowledged. Official fictions proved deadly in Vietnam, killing Americans just as much as Viet Cong and North Vietnamese soldiers. Even today the fictions remain, smiling in the shambles.

Under these very difficult circumstances, it is not surprising that the news media printed the official version of the war, at least until the 1968 Tet Offensive. Even in the aftermath of Tet, the media criticized the war effort only by reporting events that were inherently damaging to the official version. On January 31, 1968, the United States government's public relations campaign collapsed, as Viet Cong and North Vietnamese troops attacked nearly every important American base, every town and city of South Vietnam. All the talk of victory within reach, all the lies and all the promises were dispelled as the media printed and televised reports of enemy troops shooting their way into the American embassy in Saigon and fighting a pitched battle for the ancient city of Hue, a battle that lasted for days and that destroyed most of the imperial city. All the talk that Tet was a major military defeat for the Viet Cong simply missed the point: the Viet Cong could suffer such "defeats" and still continue the war indefinitely. In fact, Tet was a major victory for the Viet Cong, because the situation was so serious that the United States military could not cover it up and the media could not ignore it. The "mindless optimism" of the military would never again be taken at face value. Instead of losing the war "in little pieces over years," Herr remarks, "we lost it fast in under a week."[13]

However, even after Tet, the news media failed to reveal many aspects of the war. For example, until the story of the My Lai massacre broke in 1969, the media had been reluctant to report the racist nature of the war, according to Knightley in *The First Casualty*. As a matter of fact, the My Lai story was uncovered not by a war correspondent in Vietnam, but by a free-lance reporter back in the United States by the name of Seymour Hersh, whose original story was later expanded in *My Lai 4*. That fact, Knightley believes, constitutes a "major indictment of the coverage of the war."[14] In addition, the media's coverage of the war dwindled drastically from 1969 until 1973, as American troops were withdrawn and the brunt of the fighting was turned over to the South Vietnamese. This proved unfortunate, because some of the heaviest fighting of the war occurred during these years, including President Nixon's intensified bombing of North Vietnam, Laos, and Cambodia. The military successfully covered up American and South Vietnamese incursions into Laos and Cambodia, a cover-up made possible by the general attitude, reflected in the media, that the war was over. This attitude was possibly reinforced by the American public's boredom with the war — the war had gone on too long; it was no longer "news." At any rate, as journalist Murray Kempton has remarked, "with a million-dollar corps of correspondents in Vietnam the war in Cambodia was kept hidden for a year."[15] Vietnam became more than ever a hidden war, as secret as the origins of American intervention, long since forgotten.

Television coverage of the war had its own special problems, which had to do with both the inherent limitations of the medium and the desire on the part of network executives to gloss over the uglier aspects of the war. By reducing the conflict to a collage of disconnected scenes flitting across a screen, television automatically distorted the war. Night after night, year after year, television brought the war into the living rooms of millions of Americans. While they dined, or discussed the day's events, Walter Cronkite announced the daily search and destroy missions, the weekly body counts. The war became a kind of eerie background music: the audio punctuated by bursts of gunfire and screaming Air Force jets, and the visual composed of burning villages and running soldiers. The images blurred, and the nightly reports from Vietnam seemed so unreal that the action could have been taking place on some Hollywood set, performed by extras all playing in a modern remake of *The Sands of Iwo Jima*. Whether television wanted to or not, it gave the American public a fictionalized, Hollywood version of America at war, ignoring the racism and the brutality of Vietnam. In fact, commercial television lessened the impact of the war whenever possible, as when a Vietnamese cameraman filmed General Nguyen Ngoc Loan's infamous shooting of a man suspected of being Viet Cong during the Tet offensive: NBC blacked out the screen for three seconds after the dead man hit the ground, so as to provide a buffer before the commercial that followed. Certainly, the sight of real death could not be allowed to interfere with the selling of consumer goods or with the quiet cocktail before dinner. "What television *really* wanted was action in which the men died cleanly and not too bloodily," Phillip Knightley remarks.[16] Or as Richard Lindley writes in an article for *Esquire,* network executives wanted the nightly news to be "cinema." And that is exactly what television became.

The record speaks for itself: the news media contributed to the making of the war's secret history. Though many journalists, Fall and Halberstam among them, wrote incisive accounts of the Vietnam conflict, they were the exceptions rather than the rule. Possibly the most penetrating piece of journalism to come out of twenty years of war was Jonathan Schell's *The Village of Ben Suc*, first published in *The New Yorker* on July 15, 1967, and later in book form. In his detailed account of "Operation Cedar Falls," Schell revealed the brutality of the American "pacification" program and demonstrated that, because of its wholesale destruction of Vietnamese society, the program was doomed to fail. Misconceived and misplanned, the pacification program played into the hands of the communists by alienating the Vietnamese people. Instead of pacified, the millions of refugees were angry — angry at the Americans.

During the second week of January, 1967, Schell witnessed American and South Vietnamese troops relocate the inhabitants of several prosperous villages in the Iron Triangle area of South Vietnam. On January 8, sixty helicopters descended on Ben Suc, and as American planes bombed the surrounding woods, the villagers were herded together in the center of the village. From among the villagers, those suspected of being Viet Cong, some for "crimes" such as having been caught hiding in their bomb shelters, were selected, bound, and separated from their families. Many of the suspects were tortured by South Vietnamese troops while American soldiers looked on. One American, somewhat embarrassed by the torture, remarked to Schell: "You see, they *do* have some — well, methods and practices that *we* are not accustomed to, that we wouldn't use if we were doing it, but the thing you've got to understand is that this is an Asian country, and their first impulse is force.... It's the Asian mind. It's completely different from what we know as the Western mind, and it's hard for us to understand. Look — they're a thousand years behind us in this place, and we're trying to educate them up to our level."[17] Continuing to "educate" the villagers, the Americans and South Vietnamese troops forced all men between 15 and 45 into helicopters and took them off to the Provincial Police Headquarters for "interrogation." The women watched helplessly, "as though their fathers, brothers, and sons had ceased to exist when they ran into the roaring helicopters."[18] Then the women were loaded into evacuation trucks and taken to a refugee camp at Phu Lai, where there was no water, shelter, or sanitary facilities. The women, children, and old men found themselves surrounded by barbed wire and armed guards, and subjected to endless propaganda tapes blaring through loud speakers — in a further effort to "educate" them. In a matter of days, these first refugees had been joined by six thousand others.

However, the relocation was only the first part of "Operation Cedar Falls." The second part called for the complete razing of the villages to "deprive the V.C. of lodging and food in this area," one American explained. "From now on, anything that moves around here is going to be automatically considered V.C. and bombed or fired on."[19] So a few days later the demolition teams arrived in Ben Suc. The soldiers poured gasoline on the houses and burned the village to the ground. Then the bulldozers went to work to

> cut their own paths across the back-yard fences, small grave-yards, and ridge fields of the village, ignoring the roads and lanes. When the demolition teams withdrew, they had flattened the village, but the original plan for the demolition had not yet run its course. Faithful to the initial design, Air Force jets sent their bombs down on the deserted ruins, scorching again the burned foundations of the houses and pulverizing for a second time the heaps of rubble in the hope of collapsing tunnels too deep and well hidden

for the bulldozers to crush — as though, having once decided to destroy it, we were now bent on annihilating every possible indication that the village of Ben Suc had ever existed.[20]

The village of Ben Suc had been pacified into a wasteland.

The destruction of Ben Suc becomes, in Schell's final paragraph, a metaphor for America's attempt to destroy Vietnamese history. By attacking the family and the village, the pacification program shattered the central units of Vietnamese society, stripping the Vietnamese people from their land, their ancestors, and their past. By turning entire villages into "free-fire zones," the Americans attempted to annihilate Vietnamese culture and history so that they might more easily construct their own, much as they erected the shanty town at Phu Lai.

Schell's insights are rare, not only among the journalists, but also among the creators of novels, personal narratives, and films that have come out of the war. In general, the news media abetted the eradication of history in Vietnam.

Chapter 5. Literary Distortions

The Green Berets, et al.

> *The Green Berets* doesn't count; that
> wasn't about Vietnam, it was about
> Santa Monica. — Michael Herr,
> *Dispatches.*

Official distortions, repeated and magnified by the news media, also made their way into the literature of the Vietnam War. Of the Vietnam books that repeat official distortions, Robin Moore's *The Green Berets* provides the best example. Whereas other Vietnam novels simply allow official misrepresentations of the war by not challenging them, *The Green Berets* actually participates in the same platitudinous unrealities that characterized many American officials in Saigon. Rather than illuminating his subject, Moore obscures it in clichés.

Comparing Robin Moore to Graham Greene is useful only in that I suspect *The Green Berets* more nearly reflects public consciousness of the Vietnam War than does *The Quiet American*. Not only was *The Green Berets* (1965) the first American novel to be written about the war, it remains the only Vietnam novel or personal narrative ever to appear on the *New York Times* bestseller list. The book, and the movie version starring John Wayne, assuredly did more to shape American public opinion of the war than all the writings of Bernard Fall, for example. Moore, in fact, makes grandiose claims for his novel, which he considers a "true portrayal" of the activities of Green Beret forces in Vietnam. "*The Green Berets* is a book of truth," he writes in the preface. "I decided I could present the truth better and more accurately in the form of fiction."[1] His claim of "truth," though utter nonsense, raises serious questions and demands that his novel be evaluated according to the accuracy of its portrayal of the political and historical realities of the Vietnam War — Moore's own criteria.

Like American officials, and like the news media, Moore ignores the history of the conflict he claims to portray truthfully. He writes off the historical origins of the conflict, and two thousand years of Vietnamese history, observing that "In January of 1964 South Vietnam was being run by a military junta headed by General Buong Van ('Big') Minh that had overthrown the dictatorship of President Ngo Dinh Diem. President Diem came to power in 1955 after Vietnam was divided into two separate states — North Vietnam and South Vietnam" (p.11). How Diem, or for that matter Minh, "came to power" never enters into Moore's discussion. Neither does he give any indication of when and by whom Vietnam was "divided," an omission that makes the division sound as if it were a well established geopolitical boundary from time immemorial. Likewise, Moore ignores the fact that Vietnam was in the midst of a radical social revolution following the collapse of the French empire in Indochina, including an internal political struggle between the forces of nationalism and those elements within Vietnamese society that wanted to maintain colonial ties with the Western powers. Ho Chi Minh came to represent Vietnamese nationalism, just as Diem and other generals who had served the French in one capacity or another came to represent Vietnamese dependence. Instead, Moore reduces the conflict to outside aggression on the part of "ferocious, suicidal Communists," descending from the North like a latter-day army of Genghis Kahn. Moore portrays a Manichean conflict, in which the forces of good struggle with the forces of evil, which in this case translates into "us" versus "the Communists." Consistently labelling the North Vietnamese and the Viet Cong as "the Communists," Moore effectively blurs all finer distinctions. Like Alden Pyle's "mental concepts" in *The Quiet American*, Moore's abstractions deny the

North Vietnamese and the Viet Cong both their reality and their humanity. The consequence of the denial is the absence of moral vision in *The Green Berets.*

The key to moral vision, Peter Marin argues, comes down to "the capacity to understand two elusive truths: first, that our actions occur in a real world and have immeasurable consequences for countless others, and second, that those others are also real — not emblems, not symbols, not abstractions, not even merely 'Vietnamese' or 'Iranians' or 'Communists' or 'militants' — but concrete persons in specific situations, men and women with lives and needs as real as our own."[2] Moore's blindness reduces "the Communists" to the status of beasts to be exterminated by the Green Berets, who like Alden Pyle consider themselves to be "serving the cause of freedom around the world" (p.339). Perhaps Moore's morality can be summarized as the only good communist is a dead communist.

Following in the footsteps of Alden Pyle, Moore's Green Berets still struggle to create that mythical "third force" in Vietnamese politics, this time under the banner of General Minh. Moore's assessment of the prospects for success prove no less optimistic than Pyle's, the original quiet American. According to Moore, the Green Berets, or Special Forces, formed in 1952, can "trace its lineage back to the guerrilla operating teams of the oss (predecessor of the Central Intelligence Agency or CIA)" (p.8). (Ironically, these same oss troops trained and equipped, and fought alongside, Ho Chi Minh's own guerrillas in the waning days of World War II, as mentioned earlier.) With its illustrious background, and its dedicated soldiers right out of the Old West, Moore portrays his Green Berets as "a potent new weapon against the Communist 'war of liberation'" (p.339). However, in retrospect the "green bennie" does not seem so potent, and the fantasy of Robin Moore remains simply that, a fantasy.

One bit of dialogue illustrates the simplicity of Moore's "true portrayal," a dialogue between a Frenchman and a member of the Green Berets by the name of Scharne, though his name hardly matters since all Moore's Green Berets are one-dimensional variations of the "tough guy" stereotype — he can no more see the Americans as individuals than he can the Vietnamese. The Frenchman asks Scharne why he and his compatriots risk their lives so far away from home "for these people who steal most of what you give them and are afraid to fight for their own country" (p.149). The question assumes that the South Vietnamese, corrupt and lazy and somehow not worthy of the Americans' efforts, are in fact hampering America's fight for freedom and democracy, as if a democratic government could be established in Vietnam *despite* the Vietnamese people.

The Green Beret's response reveals even more: "First, I am a professional soldier and I take orders and do what I am told. Second, I don't want my children fighting the Communists at home" (p.149). The abstraction is essential because when one replaces "the Communists" with "the North Vietnamese" or "the Viet Cong," the entire statement is seen to be absurd. As if Ho Chi Minh had territorial ambitions in Southern California — perhaps he wanted to visit Disneyland, or to own the Los Angeles Rams? Michael Herr paid Moore the most fitting tribute in his own Vietnam book, *Dispatches. The Green Berets* "doesn't count" as a book about the Vietnam War: "That wasn't really about Vietnam, it was about Santa Monica."[3]

Many other Vietnam novels also misrepresent the war, but in slightly different ways than *The Green Berets*. In particular, the "big" naturalistic Vietnam novels, modelled on the World War II fiction of Norman Mailer and James Jones, inevitably fall back on clichés in their unsuccessful attempts to capture the complexities of Vietnam. As the most representative of these novels, William Turner Huggett's *Body Count* (1973) and Winston Groom's *Better Times Than These* (1978), demonstrate the inherent limitations of superimposing an old war-story formula on the experience of Vietnam.[4] The broad sweeping plot, the enormous cast of characters, and the detailed descriptions of combat all seem anachronistic here — from another time, another place. Huggett's and Groom's characters could and should be fighting Indians on the plains of Nebraska, or Nazis on the beaches of Normandy, not the Viet Cong in the jungles of Vietnam. In its review of *Better Times Than These, Newsweek* correctly criticized the novel for the fact that "the plot, the characters and the prose are strictly World War II surplus."[5] One could add that they aren't even good World War II surplus.

In addition to being anachronistic, these Vietnam novels are unable to present more than a surface description of the conflict. In 500 pages of purposeless action, neither *Better Times Than These* nor *Body Count* ever explores the political, historical, or moral complexities of the Vietnam War. Like *The Green Berets*, these novels fail to provide even an elusive glimpse of the historical background of the war, or of the social realities of the Vietnamese people — as if the war was fought in a vacuum, without politics, without history. Hawkins, the unlikely protagonist of *Body Count*, drops out of the Ph.D. program at Princeton (of all places), joins the Marine Corps, and goes to Vietnam because "*it's there. And I want to experience it.*"[6] Huggett attempts to eliminate any need on his part to portray the problematic nature of the war by insisting, through his characters, that the issues the war raised are ultimately unknowable: "what if we are wrong? What if we are 'imperialistic aggressors' as Arnie says? How in hell does Arnie know? How does anybody know?" — Huggett frees his characters to "go over there and get in the arena" (p.32) and in-dulge in fantasy war games. The novel's plodding, mechanical plot chronicles Hawkins' initiation into the savagery of war. As the novel progresses from one gratuitously violent scene to another, Hawkins degenerates into "an insane animal" who becomes "crazed with the kill orgy" (p.429). Huggett describes Hawkins leading his men into battle with such clichés that the passage could have been taken from *The Green Berets.* Screaming "Killlll. Kill the Sons a Bitches," Hawkins "leaped into the air screaming, and hurled the grenade. He whipped off the shotgun and fired from the half-crouch. A jolt of electricity went into the men; like machines suddenly turned on, they charged. Their voices rolled in wild yells. Madness seized them" (p.417). For Hawkins, who wallows in this "savage dance of killing," there is "no greater joy than in battle. *No greater joy in all the world*" (p.430). In fact, Hawkins loves his work so much that, in the novel's final superfluous battle, he realizes that he even enjoys killing "gooks": "Maybe he did like it. Was that wrong?" (p.439), he asks. Neither he nor his creator seem to be able to answer that question.

Better Times Than These follows the same pattern, in that Groom's protagonist (Kahn) becomes personally disillusioned with his experience in Vietnam but retreats into the argument that the war was incomprehen-sible. "Anybody who hadn't been there probably wouldn't know what in hell you were talking about,"[7] Kahn says at the end of the novel, rationalizing both his and Groom's silence, their inability to comprehend the war. In fact, Groom discredits all those who would question the war and thereby attempt to make it intelligible. For example, the characters in his novel who oppose the war all turn out to be either "political science professors," dilletantish liberals who flit from cocktail parties to antiwar demonstrations, or unfaithful girlfriends who sleep with "political science professors" while their boyfriends fight and die in Vietnam. Only such silly, wishful and deceitful intellectuals question the war. Thus Huggett and Groom both argue for the impossibility of understanding the war, possibly to compensate for their failure as novelists to provide any in-sight into a Vietnam. These writers allow official distortions of the war by abdicating any critical perspective that would have challenged them.

The absurdist novels of the Vietnam War, impoverished imitations of Joseph Heller's *Catch-22*, are worse. Two of them, James Park Sloan's *War Games* (1971) and Joe W. Haldeman's *War Year* (1972), provide ap-propriate examples. Though ostensibly "about" Vietnam, *War Games* reduces the war to the protagonist's problems with securing dental care, a suntan, and a cure for his recurring bouts with the clap. Likewise, *War Year* concerns itself with beer drinking rather than the war, as if the war were simply an excuse to drink beer in Southeast Asia. Not that these novels use Vietnam as a background for their stories: they have no stories to tell, only disconnected scenes of their characters wallowing in a frivolous, pointless absurdity. As imitators of Joseph Heller, both writers miss the point — the absurdity of *Catch-22* arises from the fact that Heller's characters are trapped in a waste land ruled by a military-economic bureaucracy as inhuman as it is insane, a bureacracy that profits from the deaths of its own men. In contrast, the absurdity of these novels results from the writers' inability to write fiction. These novels are not entertaining, they have no "literary" value, and they do not even attempt to illuminate any aspect of the war. One can only imagine the conflict of taste with commercial judgment at the publishing houses that published them. By their obsessive pointlessness, they further mystify.

Another novel, which I can only describe as an absurdist fable, shares some of the same problems as *War Games* and *War Year*. Asa Baber sets his novel, *The Land of a Million Elephants*, in a mythical kingdom called Chanda, a kingdom that is obviously meant to resemble Vietnam before the American-Indochina War. According to the dust jacket, Chanda has recently had the misfortune of being "occupied by the diplomatic and military personnel (war-loving, Unharmonious) of numerous countries, the United States among them. But there are some Harmonious people in Chanda too (The Crew). They are led by the opium-smoking, elephant-training wise man, Buon Kong, who knows more about freedom and gentleness and love of life than any other living man."[8] The novel follows the fairy tale (which is to say comic book) exploits of Buon Kong: as the Russians and the Americans jockey for power and influence, debating the expedience of intervention in Chanda, Buon Kong leads his followers on a retreat to the "Plain of Elephants," where they refuse to play politics with either of the superpowers. The Russian ambassador laments: "How can the confrontation of the Twentieth Century be brought to conclusion in dialectic terms if we have no people to sway? It would all be quite meaningless" (p.127). The Americans, not as passive as the Russians, try to bomb "The Crew" into submission, but the Chanda flower-children are protected by the spirits of the old country (the *"phi"*), and the Americans are defeated. Everyone, it seems, lives happily ever after.

Though there are some interesting details in *The Land of a Million Elephants*, the novel has the overall effect of a cartoon. The Harmonious struggle against the Unharmonious much as Popeye struggles against Bluto, both sides clearly and simplistically defined. And just when the Harmonious appear doomed, the wise man steps in with his magic and saves the day. With his opium, his elephants, and his sayings, Buon Kong resembles a 1960s drug-cult guru, a comix pied piper leading his followers into a neverneverland where the spirits always protect and the good guys always win. Baber seems to imply that if everyone would have followed his or her guru to the "Plain of Elephants," the war would have disappeared. Such nonsense seems almost obscene when applied to the Vietnam War.

Certainly, no one desiring to understand the complexity of the Vietnam War would take any of these novels seriously—but that is part of the problem. Books like *The Green Berets*, and there are many of them, all contribute to the misunderstanding of a crucially important event. Paradoxically, these books, though politically naive or totally apolitical, often make powerful public statements too often accepted as fact by popular audiences. Intentionally or unintentionally, all these books perpetuate the same kinds of erroneous political assumptions found in *The Green Berets*. Because they fail to provide a critical perspective that would make the events they describe intelligible, they allow and in fact reinforce official distortions of the war.

Chapter 6. The Dope and Dementia Theory

Dispatches and Other Evasions

> *A sense of unreality is not a legal defense.* — Robert Stone, *Dog Soldiers.*

Drugs and rock-and-roll suffuse the writing that has come out of the Vietnam War. "Rock-and-roll madness" serves as a recurring theme in a profoundly nihilistic body of literature, in which a sense of unreality is the literary terrain. Often portraying the war as a descent into insanity, this literature promotes what Zalin Grant has referred to as the "dope and dementia interpretation of Vietnam."[1] Thus Mark Baker, for example, can liken the war to a kind of nightmarish fairy tale: "Vietnam was a brutal Neverneverland, outside time and space, where little boys did not have to grow up. They just grew old before their time."[2] But the Vietnam War was *not* a cartoon or a fairy tale, nor was it outside history. The novels and personal narratives that dwell in this "Never-neverland" further obscure an event already obscure in the minds of most Americans.

After so many years of official propaganda, the war understandably seemed incomprehensible to many people. Rational analysis collided with the government's massive public relations campaign to sell the war, a campaign built on exaggerated statistics and falsified progress reports. When American officials could no longer conceal the truth about Vietnam, and when official fiction finally collapsed, the political realities of the war had become so muddled that very few people were able to put the pieces back together in a coherent whole. For one thing, few people possessed the historical knowledge needed to make sense of a war as steeped in historical connection as Vietnam. In fact, few people even knew that United States intervention in Vietnam extended as far back as 1950, when the Truman administration began funding the French military effort in Vietnam, siding with the French colonialists against Vietnamese nationalism. So much of that history remained unknown that the war seemed to have been a sudden, mysterious eruption of hostilities. Five different American presidents and their administrations tried to make the history of the war secret. The United States government made the war unintelligible, but for politically intelligible reasons— that is, to sell a war that needed selling, both from a pragmatic and a moral standpoint.

The Vietnam books that project the "dope and dementia" theory mirror this cultural confusion. The authors experienced the insanity of the war first hand, all of them having served in Vietnam in some capacity, either in the military, the news media, or both. Their accounts abound with scenes of nightmarish horror, and they share a hallucinatory ambience that distinguishes them from the literature of past wars, a psychedelic quality that infects the characters and the stories and converts the war into "a play in giddy senselessness," as William Eastlake writes in *The Bamboo Bed*. *Catch-22* serves as a model for this literature, except that Heller's absurdist tone differs significantly from the more violent, hallucinatory tone of the Vietnam books. Yossarian's night of horror in "The Eternal City" chapter of *Catch-22* comes closest to the experiences of these latter-day protagonists caught in a nightmare from which they cannot awake: 365 days in "No Man's Nam." Unlike *Catch-22*, however, very little humor offsets the horrifying vision of the Vietnam books, and what humor does exist is usually so black as to be in-distinguishable from the pain and horror, a kind of insane cackling. The Vietnam books, almost without exception, fail to arrive at Yossarian's partial reconciliation at the end of *Catch-22*: the affirmation of life, in spite of everything. Hawkins, Charles Durden's narrator in *No Bugles*,

No Drums, confesses his reaction upon first reading *Catch-22*: "I said this dude's gotta be crazy. He was. But he wasn't crazy enough. ... Maybe everybody's war is the worst. But I'm here to tell you, sports fans, if the next one is any more fucked up than this one I don't want to know nothin' from nothin'."[3]

In its portrait of the unreality of the war, Michael Herr's *Dispatches* stands as the most representative of all the "dope and dementia" Vietnam books. Critics have widely praised the literary merits of the narrative. For example, Pearl K. Bell referred to it as the "most consciously and ornately literary book about Vietnam."[4] Reviewers compared it to the best American writing to come out of any war, and C.D.B. Bryan wrote in the *New York Times Book Review* that "quite simply, *Dispatches* is the best book to have been written about the Vietnam War."[5] And yet in spite of its stylistic brilliance, *Dispatches* suffers from serious failures as a work of war reporting, failures that Herr even admits to. "Talk about impersonating an identity, about locking into a role, about irony; I went to cover the war and the war covered me,"[6] Herr writes near the beginning, providing a clue as to how this material managed to elude him, to slip through his consciousness without ever being assembled into coherence. As a veteran correspondent in Vietnam, Herr had the opportunity to make *Dispatches* more than just a personal narrative of the war; his going in and out of combat by helicopter could have become a metaphor for the kind of literary response that would have rendered Vietnam more truly — the kind of book that would have described the "inner" war on the ground, but that also would have allowed the writer the overview needed to place events in historical perspective. *Dispatches* succeeds as "the journey of its author through his own consciousness," as John Hellman argues in "The New Journalism and Vietnam."[7] However, the book fails to transcend the limits of its self-reflexive stance, and Herr himself admits having fallen victim to the "problem" that Vietnam presents for so many Americans unable to extricate themselves from their own confusion. The "problem," Herr writes, "was that you didn't always know what you were seeing until later, maybe years later, that a lot of it never made it in at all, it just stayed stored there in your eyes. Time and imagination, rock and roll, life itself, the information isn't frozen, you are" (p.20). The word "frozen" provides an excellent metaphor for the inability to comprehend, to interpret, to transcend.

Herr's title is itself significant, for *Dispatches* is a book of dispatches or fragments, bits of narrative that remain diffuse and discontinuous. Lacking an overall structure, in fact denying the possibility of structure, the fragments refuse to lend themselves to interpretation, to the discovery of meaning. Herr's fragmented structure expresses the surreality of the war stories he spins out, laced with death and annihilation, with acid rock blaring in the background. Like so many others, Herr could not avoid "losing" himself in the war: "All right, yes, it had been a groove being a war correspondent, hanging out with the grunts and getting close to the war, touching it, losing yourself in it and trying yourself against it" (p.251). It would be interesting to know exactly what he means by "a groove."

Herr despairs of ever understanding the war. For example, though he mentions its "secret history," he never bothers to clarify that secret history. In fact, he further obfuscates the origins of the war when he writes: "you couldn't find two people who agreed about when it began, how could you say when it began going off?" (p.49). And: "might as well say that Vietnam was where the Trail of Tears was headed all along ... might as well lay it on the proto-Gringos who found the New England woods too raw and empty for their peace and filled them up with their own imported devils" (p.49). Perhaps the Americans did fill Vietnam with their own imaginary devils, but surely a more precise explanation is possible. Herr's remote interpretation makes the war seem as natural as Thanksgiving.

Similarly, when discussing the reasons for United States intervention in Vietnam, Herr retreats into a sarcasm that further mystifies the war. In Vietnam all the Americans were "true volunteers," Herr writes: "Not that you didn't hear some overripe bullshit about it: Hearts and Minds, People of the Republic, tumbling dominos, maintaining the equilibrium of the Dingdong by containing the ever encroaching Dooday" (p.20). Also, Herr begins *Dispatches* with a description of an old map on the wall of his apartment in Saigon, a map that "wasn't real anymore": the "uses of most information were flexible," and "even the most detailed of maps didn't reveal much anymore; reading them was like trying to read the faces of the Vietnamese, and that was like trying to read the wind" (p.3). Unfortunately, Herr does not replace the wornout map with a new one.

However, one further and even more important criticism of *Dispatches* needs to be made: Herr betrays a fascination with the glamour of war, a fascination that enables him to describe young soldiers as "so innocent and violent, so sweet and so brutal, beautiful killers" (p.235). Time after time he refers to the war as "wonderful" or as a "groove." "Some people found it distasteful or confusing if I told them that, whatever else, I'd loved it there too" (p.251), he writes. Unlike Greene in *The Quiet American*, Herr refuses to take a consistent moral stance. To Herr, despite his criticisms of the war, Vietnam "had been merely wonderful" (p.244). Perhaps a comment from Herr's friend and fellow correspondent Tim Page, whom Herr quotes near the end of the book, best expresses the murky moral terrain of *Dispatches*. "Take the glamour out of war! I mean, how the bloody hell can you do *that*?" (p.248). Herr's aesthetic fascination with the war contradicts his occasional moral disgust. When he calls the war "wonderful" or glamourous, it is as if he were watching a movie.

I am not suggesting that Herr is totally wrong in his portrayal, only that he fails to go beyond a surface description, beyond the "dope and dementia" aspects. Most Vietnam books share Herr's view that the war did not make any sense, and for many of the same reasons. For example, a number of books remark on General Westmoreland's strategy of attrition, which they describe as an endless body count where success could only be measured by numbers — numbers that meant nothing at all. "Our mission was not to win terrain or seize positions, but simply to kill," Philip Caputo writes in *A Rumor of War*.[8] Caputo points out that this policy of attrition led not only to fictionalized body counts, but to an "open season" attitude toward the Vietnamese people. "If it's dead and Vietnamese, then it's Viet Cong." That rule of thumb, these books imply, brought the United States military dangerously close to a calculated policy of genocide.

Whether fiction or nonfiction, the Vietnam books present the plight of the common American soldiers who find themselves expected to fight for no other reason than to kill. And when they kill indiscriminately, in an indiscriminate war, many of these characters end up facing courts-martial or dishonorable discharges. Ironically, they face charges of murder in a war of murder, and they become confused and bitter at both the military and their own government. In one memorable incident in *Dispatches*, Herr quotes a young G.I. who asks the ultimate question: "I mean, if we can't shoot these peole, what the fuck are we doing here?" (p.29). That question has never been answered.

Philip Caputo illustrates the insanity of Westmoreland's war of numbers in "The Officer in Charge of the Dead," the second part of *A Rumor of War*. Under protest, Caputo is assigned to the rear and given the ludicrous task of keeping a running score of American and Viet Cong losses. He becomes "death's bookkeeper," posting the body counts on a giant "scoreboard" whose numbers change daily — as if the war were a football game, first and ten, life and death. But as Caputo discovers, "maintaining an accurate scoreboard" (p.160) proves essential to public relations, for it pacifies high-ranking officers from Danang and Saigon who drop in from time to time to check on the unit's performance. When the scoreboard does not suffice, Caputo's commanding officer dreams up other schemes, such as ordering him to drag dead Viet Cong bodies around the base or to leave the decomposing bodies out in plain sight for the officers to see. If not the scoreboard, then the stench of decomposing flesh provides the necessary progress reports, and Caputo remarks cynically: "In the patriotic fervor of the Kennedy years, we had asked 'What can we do for our country?' and our country answered 'Kill VC.' That was the strategy, the best our military minds could come up with: organized butchery" (p.218).

The Vietnam books portray not only the war, but the military command as insane. Men armed with "phrases in search of ideas," Josiah Bunting labels the military in *The Lionheads,* a novel that emphasizes the parasitical nature of the military bureacracy.[9] *The Lionheads* and many other books depict the military as composed of ambitious, ruthless men whose drive for promotion leads them to sacrifice their own men on dangerous missions, all to produce higher body counts. "Sometimes I think all the right people must live in little rooms, thinkin' up slogans and workin' on new numbers games so the grunts'll keep humpin' for the generals" (p.21), reflects the narrator of Charles Durden's *No Bugles, No Drums.* The "mindless optimism" of the military takes many forms in these books, all of which describe the disastrous consequences of that optimism, that derangement of the senses which sent so many American soldiers to their deaths. "Command bravado," Herr refers to it, an insane dialogue that "caused heavy casualties to be announced as light, routs and ambushes to be described as temporary tactical ploys, and filthy weather to be characterized as good and even excellent" (p.143). One colonel even explains the war to Herr in terms of "protein": "We were a nation of high-protein, meat-eating hunters, while the other guy just ate rice and a few grungy fish heads. We were going to club him to death with our meat" (p.60). What could one say except "Colonel, you're insane?" (p.60), Herr asks, commenting that talking to such people was like "turning up in the middle of some black looneytune where the Duck had all the lines" (p.60). One would be at a loss to find a favorable presentation of any of the generals or lesser officers who directed the war. One small bit of dialogue from William Eastlake's *The Bamboo Bed* expresses the consensus of these writers. "Who is the high command?" one character asks. To which another responds: "Insanity."[10]

Given this portrait of Vietnam, it hardly comes as a surprise that the desperate characters who inhabit this literature (some fictional, some real) experience the war as incomprehensible. To these characters, caught between the hostility of the civilian population and the insanity of their superiors, the war is a nightmare of horror and death. "If you have ever wondered what nowhere looks like," William Eastlake writes in *The Bamboo Bed,* "it is a monsoon-shrouded clearing in the vast jungle of Vietnam, the inhabitants of nowhere dying and surrounded by the dead" (p.50). How could they feel any differently, sleeping on little islands of safety, encircled by coils of barbed wire and minefields, surrounded by "unfriendlies" and an immense, hostile, unfamiliar countryside? Survival becomes their only victory, and many of them are even denied that (survival being the only rationale left in a totally pointless world). Consider Clancy, for example, the protagonist of *The Bamboo Bed*. Described as the "eternal warrior," as a mythical representative of all American warriors, Captain Clancy lays dying in the jungle while around him the war continues in a swirl of events that he cannot comprehend, that none of the characters in the novel can comprehend. Clancy dies, and he dies "for our sins," unable to make sense out of a senseless war.

Durden's *No Bugles, No Drums* provides perhaps the most vivid portrait of an American soldier caught in the insanity of the war. Pfc. Jamie Hawkins, Durden's narrator, has a "bad attitude" before he comes to Vietnam, but his experiences in "this misbegotten crotch of creation" (p.9) make his attitude a hell of a lot worse. Finding himself in a company assigned to guard a pig farm by the name of "Song My Swine," Hawkins thinks, "this shit was like a badly made movie. The focus was all fucked up" (p.19). Trapped in a war with his focus awry, Hawkins tries to correct it by penetrating the large absurdities that he finds everywhere in this war, fought "to contain Communism, or repel nationalism, or expand capitalism, or whatever the fuck we were s'posed to be doin' in No Man's Nam" (p.86). Hawkins asks too many questions, and one of his fellow soldiers likens him to a nine-year-old kid "who still thinks there orta be some sense t' things" (p.95). Aside from the war itself being "for nothin'," Hawkins has to contend with his commanding officers and the corporate structure of the military-industrial complex: "the fuckin' thieves, war profiteers, black-market motherfuckers, the ego-centered bigoted bastards lookin' to get promoted, jerkoffs like the colonel who gives out lovin' cups for the most VC KIA" (p.210). Needless to say, with his questions and his relentless analysis, Hawkins does not fit very well into the army.

In his efforts to make experience intelligible, or to get a "handle" on things as he says at one point, Hawkins repeatedly "confesses to his role as the observer, the listener, the note-taker, the thinker-adventurer in search of some stable, representational stance," according to Philip D. Beidler.[11] Not only does Hawkins carefully record and analyze his experience, he compares it to fiction where characters are "steadfast" and events are intelligible. But life does not resemble fiction in Vietnam, where the only permanence turns out to be unsteadfastness. As Hawkins admits, "you think you've got the handle on somethin', and then you find out there's another handle, and another" (p.37). Hawkins feels terribly alone, as his fellow soldiers have long since given up the struggle to understand, not caring whether the war was "a farce or some fuckin' far-out reality" beyond comprehension. Running on empty, so to speak, Hawkins falls back on the only device left him: the power of expression, the power to name things. For perception, Hawkins realizes, corresponds with and in fact is contingent upon expression, and so he gropes for the right words. Philip Beidler observes that the "passionate concreteness" of Hawkins' speech can be linked to an "explicit concern with the relationship between language and experiential truth."[12] Hawkins' outrageously colloquial language, supposedly a Georgia dialect, allows him to articulate his experiential gropings in very concrete terms. No matter that his friends make fun of the way he talks; only the gift of language keeps Hawkins from descending into the contagious insanity of the war.

No Bugles, No Drums chronicles Hawkins' growing disillusionment. Loosely modeled on *Catch-22*, the novel follows Hawkins to his less than honorable discharge at the end. Like Yossarian in *Catch-22*, Hawkins simply walks away from the military, wanting nothing more to do with the "Machiavellian motherfuckers." But whereas Yossarian's exit represents an affirmation of sorts, Hawkins affirms nothing but the prerogative to tell the powers-that-be to go fuck themselves. Like Herr, Hawkins fails to correct the distorted focus, fails to achieve a stance that would reveal the war in its proper perspective, and he loses his "ambitions" to "make somethin' outa life that's worth the goddamn effort" (p.142). The same thing can be said of the author, for Durden does not overcome his narrator's inability to penetrate the inscrutability of Vietnam. In fact, Durden clearly sympathizes with Hawkins' failure in his "war with the Army." Thus the novel ends on a dark note: "the only thing subject Hawkins had left was his unshakeable bad attitude" (p.287).

The problem with *Dispatches* and *No Bugles, No Drums,* and the other "dope and dementia" Vietnam books, then, is not that they call the war insane but that they let it go at that. They treat the war as unknowable and incomprehensible, as if (in Eastlake's words) it "had a momentum of its own, as though the war were sentient and alive, although born of man it now has a life separate, unremitting, without meaning, purposeless, without direction, feckless, willful and mad" (p.194). Accepting this mystification of the war, these books retreat into cynicism or a bitter sarcasm. For example, Caputo remarks in the preface of *A Rumor of War* that "this book ought not to be regarded as a protest. Protest arises from a belief that one can change things or influence events. I am not egotistical enough to believe I can" (p.xxi). Though catchy, Caputo's words illogically present the "tragifarce" of Vietnam as some kind of *condition humaine*, destined to be repeated endlessly. Herr's withdrawal at the end of *Dispatches* into the "glamour" of war constitutes another kind of cynicism, not so different from Caputo's or Durden's.

Even worse are the Vietnam books that conclude in outright sarcasm, a sarcasm as nihilistic as anything in American literature. For example, Gustav Hasford's *The Short-Timers* indulges in an overdose of surreal fantasies of carnage and machismo that become absolutely point-less: "Come one, come all to exotic Vietnam, the jewel of Asia, meet in-teresting, stimulating people of an ancient culture ... and kill them." And: "I love the little Commie bastards, man. I really do. Grunts under-stand grunts. These are great days we are living, bros. We are jolly green giants walking the earth with guns. The people wasted here today are the finest individuals we will ever know. When we rotate back to the World we're gonna miss having somebody around who's worth shooting."[13] Such escapist sarcasm does not replace a critical perspective or correct official distortions. And that, precisely, is the failure.

By now, the politics of the "dope and dementia" theory should be evident. Literary responses that retreat into "rock-and-roll madness" im-ply the impossibility of social, political, and historical understanding. The "dope and dementia" books, despite their criticisms of the war, tacitly or unwittingly acknowledge their powerlessness before such in-stitutions as the government, the military, and the media. The unspoken argument of these books would seem to be: government and media ac-counts of the war were false, therefore we can never know the truth about it. Government maps were misleading, therefore the Vietnamese landscape and culture are forever mysterious and unknowable. Govern-ment histories of the war were distorted, therefore the war's origins will never be clear. Our stated reasons for being in Vietnam were absurd; therefore we can never know why we were there (the war just appeared insanely and arbitrarily, like a sniper on a downtown building). Beyond a doubt, making sense of Vietnam *is* difficult, as so many of the Vietnam writers emphasize. However, by implying that the war is impossible to understand, these writers simply play into the hands of all those who wanted (and still want) to keep the war a mystery.

Finally, the "dope and dementia" books reflect a very serious con-temporary problem—the despair of not being able to understand exter-nal reality and history. Americans, especially, have always been reluc-tant to acknowledge social and historical connection, but recently that blindness has been taken to the extreme of total denial. If external reality depends on who perceives it, if history comes to no more than a figment of a writer's imagination, and if values are similarly subjective and ar-bitrary, then it becomes impossible for a writer (or anyone) to penetrate the meaning of experience. Thus we find ourselves irrevocably dispossessed of the ability to understand the social, political and historical realities that we inhabit, whether we choose to acknowledge them or not. Given this dead-end, Gerald Graff writes in *Literature Against Itself*, the writer's problem is "to find a standpoint from which to represent the diffuse, intransigent material of contemporary experience without surrendering critical perspective to it. Since critical perspective depends on historical sense, on seeing the present somehow as part of a coherent historical process, this task demands a difficult fusion of the sense of contemporaneity with the sense of the past."[14] In the final analysis, the "dope and dementia" theory is not equal to this task. No matter how well written, a book of rock-and-roll madness cannot by itself capture the meaning of the war. Even the most brilliant of these books convey only a part of the truth. Because of what they omit, these books display their dexterity in a moral and political void.

Chapter 7. Recovering a Secret History

One Very Hot Day and *Going After Cacciato*

> But then historical memory was never
> the forte of Americans in Vietnam. —
> Frances Fitzgerald, *Fire in the Lake.*

The "real key" to understanding the Vietnam War, David Halber-stam wrote in a letter to Phillip Knightley, was the fact that "it was all derivative of the French Indo-China War, which is history." In Vietnam, Halberstam argued, "we were haunted and indeed imprisoned by the past."[1] For 21 years, from 1955 to 1975, United States forces in Vietnam walked in the footsteps of the French and yet apparently learned nothing from the obvious connection. American officials did their best to deny history, and the news media simply ignored it. Similarly, very few Vietnam writers make use of this historical "key" in their efforts to unlock the meaning of Vietnam.

The three most highly praised personal narratives of the war —
Michael Herr's *Dispatches*, Philip Caputo's *A Rumor of War*, and Ron
Kovic's *Born on the Fourth of July* — do not attempt to place the war in
historical perspective. Herr mentions that the United States government
and the news media participated in making the history of the war
"secret," but never bothers to restore the history to us. Both Caputo and
Kovic blame the war on illusions and false idealism generated by
President Kennedy, whom Caputo refers to as a "political witch doctor."
However, instead of history, these writers give us their own fictions,
which effectively dehistoricize the war, the origin of which certainly
predates Kennedy's "Camelot" years. The Vietnam novels do not fare
much better than the personal narratives, when considered in their entirety. Totally lacking a historical dimension, most of the novels present
the war in terms of how it affects their protagonists personally. When
mentioned at all, history becomes a ghostly presence, an abandoned
French armored vehicle or a ruined watchtower that serves as a reminder
of possible failure. The three notable exceptions are William Eastlake's
The Bamboo Bed, David Halberstam's *One Very Hot Day*, and Tim
O'Brien's National Book Award winning novel, *Going After Cacciato*.

In *The Bamboo Bed* (1969), William Eastlake transforms the particular history of Vietnam into a recurring, mythical confrontation. Captain Clancy, Eastlake's version of the American Hero, comes to Vietnam
as the "eternal warrior." Raised in a militaristic society, weaned on
imaginary war games as a child, Clancy plays a Vietnamese version of
cowboys and Indians. When not making war, Clancy makes love to
Madame Dieudonné, a French woman who lives in an underground villa
on an old rubber plantation. Eastlake likens the underground villa to a
"grave" and he presents Madame Dieudonné as the "eternal whore":
death. In Eastlake's mythic scheme, the "eternal warrior" and the "eternal
whore" "were bound to come together in Vietnam" — they coupled when
the French entered the dark jungle of Vietnam, and later when the
Americans made the same mistake. In fact, Eastlake draws explicit
parallels between the French and American Indochina wars; "visiting a
grave" and fornicating with the "eternal whore" become metaphors for
both interventions in Vietnam. Clancy dies on a hill called "Ridge Red
Boy," just as Madame Dieudonné's husband and so many other French-
men died on their own hills. "Where do I go now? Where does anyone go
now from the day of our dead?" one of Clancy's men asks. The response
is like a refrain: "They go to Dien Bien Phu. They go to Ridge Red
Boy."[2] History recurs, Eastlake implies — and for all the "eternal warriors"
and all the "tinhorn Custer[s]," "Vietnam waits."

A much more realistic novel, *One Very Hot Day* (1967) was one of
the first important Vietnam novels written by an American. Like *The*

Quiet American, the novel evoked angry responses at the time of its publication and many critics attacked the book as an antiwar novel. Concerned with the early part of the war when Americans were serving only as "advisers" to the South Vietnamese, the novel does not descend into surrealism or absurdity as do so many later Vietnam novels. Halberstam succeeds in providing a critical perspective with which to interpret the war, setting his novel in a social and historical context that he knew well, having lived and worked as a journalist in Vietnam for a number of years. His novel serves as an illustration of his comment to Phillip Knightley that history provided the "real key" to understanding Vietnam.

Captain Beaupre, the protagonist of *One Very Hot Day,* finds himself too old at the age of 38 for a war that was "all too modern for him."[3] For Beaupre, the war consists of endless missions, long hot walks in the sun in search of an enemy that always remains one village ahead, pointless interrogations of old men and women who "hate our guts," who "would as soon kill us as look at us" (p.64). Even when they succeed in finding the enemy, the Vietnamese soldiers more often than not refuse to fight — and why shouldn't they? They do not want to serve the Americans any more than the villagers do. "Just hiking each day with death, taking chances for so very little" (p.125) has totally disillusioned Beaupre. He drowns his sorrow in alcohol every night, and he goes whoring in Saigon almost every weekend. In fact, Beaupre is known as "the only man in My Tho who will risk five ambushes for one hairless Indo-Chinese piece of ass" (p.97).

On every mission Beaupre and his fellow Americans walk in the footsteps of the French: "wondering if [they] were going to be sold out, wondering whom you could trust" (p.126). But Beaupre blames the war itself, not the Vietnamese people; he knows only too well that few Vietnamese will risk their lives for the American government in Saigon. Those like Lieutenant Thuong who serve in the South Vietnamese Army have been "corrupted" by their collaboration. Thuong, for example, envies the Viet Cong their "self-belief, their ideology, their certainty, even their cruelty" (p.131). Suspecting that the war will be lost, he "has no illusions, and he knows that the Viet Cong are just as cruel as the French or the Americans, but without the corruption" (p.132). He does not defect to the Viet Cong because "he knew he was too cynical for the passion and commitment their life took" (p.132). The Americans, too, had been "corrupted" by their involvement in Vietnam, Thuong realizes. At first, "he had believed they would work and that *they could change what no one else could change;* they did not, after all, lose wars, that was well known in all the history books ... and they were big and rich (much richer, he knew, than the French)" (p.45). But later he realized that "instead of changing Vietnam, they were changing with it, and becoming part of it; until finally he was more aware of their frailties than he was of Vietnamese frailties" (p.45). "The myth of the Americans was once and forever ended," Thuong says, "and they were ... at the very least a fallible people" (p.46). Locked into the footsteps of the French, the Americans and their South Vietnamese allies have taken on the sins of the harbingers.

One central passage in the novel reveals just how the Americans have been "corrupted" by their own actions in Vietnam. With his usual touch of sarcasm, Beaupre compares the Americans to the leeches sucking the blood from a fellow officer's legs: "They've read all their publicity and their history books, got themselves sure as hell brainwashed, and they see themselves not as blood suckers, not that at all, but as life savers" (p.138). Beaupre laughs at the American leeches who believe their own propaganda, who believe they are in Vietnam "to save lives," when in fact they are draining the life-blood of Vietnam.

Halberstam's novel has a simple yet effective structure: the action takes place on one very hot day, on a mission that leads Beaupre and his men to a final, disastrous encounter with the Viet Cong. Suspense mounts as they enter one hostile village after another, and the day grows hotter, as if to mock them. When the Viet Cong attack in the very last chapter of the novel, most of the patrol are killed instantly. Beaupre, however, survives, and he looks out at the dead "scattered in all directions, as if someone with a giant hand had rolled them out like dice" (p.195). Beaupre takes charge and forces the South Vietnamese soldiers to return fire, but afterward, exhausted and more disillusioned than ever, he reflects on the futility of the war. Beaupre objects to the war on pragmatic and historical grounds — the Viet Cong will win eventually, no matter what the Americans do. The Viet Cong will win because they are better soldiers; they have won before, and they have the support of the Vietnamese people, at least more support than the Saigon government has. "What a goddamm silly business to die here," Beaupre thinks, "surrounded by soldiers like this as if it were really a great joke, not even a war" (p.178). The war has become "just a long walk in the sun" (p.68), as senseless and futile as its destination in sudden, random death. Tomorrow would be another long walk in the sun, the next day another. It is, Beaupre concludes, a "lousy goddamn war" (p.88).

In contrast, Tim O'Brien approaches the history of the Vietnam War in an entirely different way. Though not as explicitly historical as *One Very Hot Day*, O'Brien's *Going After Cacciato* (1978) explores the problem that arises from the absence of historical perspective. He portrays the confusion of his young American soliders sent to Vietnam with no social or historical understanding of the Vietnamese people. His characters find themselves thrown into a war they can not understand, whose reasons for fighting remain as inaccessible as Vietnamese culture. Short-timers all of them, they live day to day with no understanding of the war: "they knew nothing about Vietnam, or what was happening in the war, or what had happened a year ago. They did not see themselves as men who had burst into history,"[4] Gloria Emerson writes in *Winners and Losers,* a statement that perfectly defines the dilemma of O'Brien's characters in *Going After Cacciato.* By obscuring the history of the war, their own government has denied them the knowledge with which to understand Vietnam. Denied comprehension, they are unable to make intelligible a war that most of them accordingly come to regard as a descent into madness. Instead of history, they have burst into insanity.

Pfc. Paul Berlin, O'Brien's young protagonist, represents all the young men confused by a confusing war. An 18-year-old farm boy from Iowa, Berlin "was scared, yes, and confused and lost, and he had no sense of what was expected of him or of what to expect from himself."[5] In a brilliant chapter entitled "The Things They Didn't Know," O'Brien provides a moving portrait of the plight of Berlin and his fellow grunts. The chapter reads like a chant: "Not knowing the language, they did not know the people.... Not knowing the people, they did not know friends from enemies" (pp.263-64). The chapter concludes with a paragraph as fine as any writing to have come out of the Vietnam War, or any war for that matter:

> They did not know even the simple things: a sense of victory, or satisfaction, or necessary sacrifice. They did not know the feeling of taking a place and keeping it, securing a village and then raising the flag and calling it a victory. No sense of order or momentum. No front, no rear, no trenches laid out in neat parallels. No Patton rushing for the Rhine, no beachheads to storm and win and hold for the duration. They did not have targets. They did not have a cause. They did not know if it was a war of ideology or economics or hegemony or spite. ... They did not know good from evil [pp.272-73].

Paul Berlin did not know which speeches to believe, which books, which politicians. He did not know who really started the war, or why, or when. He had gone to war for reasons "beyond knowledge": because going to war was expected of him, and because he did not want to risk censure. Not that he had anything against the Vietnamese, who like him were victims of "forces beyond reckoning," of "high-level politics." No, in fact he "wanted them to understand, all of them, that he felt no hate. It was all a sad accident, he would have told them — chance, high-level politics, confusion" (p.265). Above all, he wanted them to understand that he was just as trapped, just as "injured" as they were. His intentions were "benign," he pleads with them silently to understand, trying to convince himself of his own innocence. He and the others were trapped fighting a war they did not believe in, fighting an enemy they had nothing against. As a result, "they fought the war, but no one took sides" (p.272).

Berlin's disbelief in the war, and his attempt to justify his participation, produce a kind of schizophrenia that Doc (the squad medic) refers to as "fear biles." Doc lists the physical symptoms as a "numbness of the extremities in times of extremity; a cloudiness of vision; paralysis of the mental processes that separate what is truly happening from what only might have happened" (p.29). "Infecting the brain" and "fucking up reality," the fear bile works as a mental blocking device to enable Berlin to cope with the nightmarish terror of the war. This coping takes the form of an act of the imagination, by which Berlin attempts to dissociate himself from the reality of the war. During a night of guard duty, Berlin dreams (we discover as the novel progresses) the desertion of Cacciato, who simply walks away from the war with the avowed intention of making his way to Paris, 8,600 miles away. The 3rd Squad follows Cacciato, though whether to bring him back or desert with him never becomes clear. The novel, then, builds on a point-counter-point structure, with the imaginary pursuit of Cacciato juxtaposed with chapters recounting Berlin's night of guard duty and his debate as to whether they could make it all the way to Paris. "With courage it might have been done" (p.325), Berlin tries to convince himself, though he never quite succeeds.

The problem is that Berlin's imagination keeps brushing up against reality, just as the imaginary progress reports of military and State department officials kept smashing against the reality of Vietnam. The 3rd Squad confronts repeated obstacles that threaten to derail their escape from the war. As their imaginary journey takes them farther away from Vietnam, they experience a series of encounters that inevitably bring them back to the war: a North Vietnamese officer who tells them that their true enemy in Vietnam is the land, where a man's spirit abides and "where his ancestors rest and where the rice grows" (p.86); a SAVAC officer in Iran who tells them that all soldiers will run without "purpose," that they "will act out their dreams, and they will run and run, like animals in stampede" (p.200). When they arrive in Paris, Berlin's imagination fails them — he cannot project an end, a way out, a resolution. Instead, they succumb to duty and attempt to capture Cacciato, planning an ambush on his hotel room on the "Fontaine des Innocents." However, they find the room empty, and the dream comes to a sudden, violent end: Berlin goes temporarily insane, firing his M-16 until the room becomes a black, burning emptiness. When he regains his senses, Berlin finds himself back at the hill where Cacciato had disappeared, with Doc and the others comforting him. Imagination fails, because "imagination, like reality, has its limits" (p.323).

Arthur M. Saltzman has argued that in *Going After Cacciato* O'Brien "recognizes the soldier's need to cling to something," which he defines as "duty" and "self-respect."[6] However, I find that O'Brien recognizes the need of these soldiers not to cling to, but to dissociate themselves from, an intolerable situation, however doomed their efforts might be. Reality asserts itself over imagination as it of course must, but only the "official" or distorted reality that has made the war incomprehensible. Berlin and the 3rd Squad can only fall back on concepts such as "duty" and "self-respect" — which are, ironically, the very concepts that entrapped them in the first place. This becomes clear in a scene that comes right before the attempted capture of Cacciato, where Berlin and a Vietnamese woman by the name of Sarkin Aung Wan participate in an imaginary recreation of the Paris peace talks (it is hardly a coincidence that Cacciato and crew dreamwalk to Paris, where the peace talks promise another imaginary end to the war, the quest serving as a kind of wish-fulfillment). Sitting at a large circular table in the Majestic Hotel, Berlin representing the United States, Sarkin representing the Democratic Republic of Vietnam, the two negotiators state their positions without looking at one another. Sarkin speaks first: "Do not be frightened by ridicule or censure or embarrassment, do not fear name-calling, do not fear the scorn of others. For what is true obligation? Is it not the obligation to pursue a life at peace with itself? ... I urge you: March proudly into your own dreams" (pp.320-21), she concludes. Then Berlin speaks: "We all want peace. We all want dignity and domestic tranquility. But we want these to be honorable and lasting. We want a peace that endures. We want a peace we can live with. We want a peace we can be proud of" (p.323). Even in his imagination, Berlin retreats into official slogans and platitudes, unable to either imaginatively or intellectually transcend the propaganda of his own government. Berlin can no more escape his own confusion than his government can.

Going After Cacciato illustrates how official distortions of the war proved self-defeating for the United States. By making history secret, the government made the war unintelligible to its own people, and it ended up pursuing unrealistic objectives that a knowledge of the past would have exposed as futile. Lacking self-evident reasons, denied historical perspective, the American soldiers sent to fight the war "were not committed, not resigned, to having to win a war," O'Brien writes in his own personal memoir, *If I Die in a Combat Zone,*[8] earlier in the 1970's. From his own experiences in Vietnam, O'Brien found that patriotism itself had come to be regarded as nothing less than insanity: "Horace's old do-or-die aphorism — 'Dulce et decorum est pro patria mori' — was just an epitaph for the insane." So, ironically, the secret history of this secret war worked against those who had made it. And in the end, in David Halberstam's words, "we were haunted and indeed imprisoned by the past" for the simple reason that we made no effort to acknowledge or understand it. History cannot be so easily denied.

Chapter 8. Moral Explorations

The Prisoners of Quai Dong and *Dog Soldiers*

> *But organized or not, butchery was*
> *butchery, so who was to speak of rules*
> *and ethics in a war that had none? —*
> Philip Caputo, *A Rumor of War.*

Of the more than fifty novels and personal narratives that have been written about the Vietnam War, only a handful ever discuss the questionable morality of it. That fact seems rather surprising at first, especially in light of the intense national debate over that issue beginning in the mid and late 1960s. However, approximately three-fourths of these books were published during the 1970s, and I suspect that their reluctance to broach moral concerns reflects a culture that grew increasingly disillusioned and apathetic during that bitter decade, a culture that found and still finds it difficult to discuss a subject as apparently subjective as morality. For morality depends on human values, and all such values are merely personal and subjective, or so the argument goes. Thus moral questions remain unanswered today, repressed in the human mind, hidden in the rubble of the late 20th century. The fear of morality haunts us like the spectre of Vietnam itself.

Unlike Graham Greene in *The Quiet American*, most American writers deny the possibility of moral responsibility in a war as problematic as Vietnam. "We all had roughly the same position on the war," Michael Herr writes: "we were in it, and that was a position."[1] Tim O'Brien arrives at more or less the same "position" in his memoir, *If I Die in a Combat Zone*. Though convinced the war was "wrong" for various reasons that "could be murmured like the Psalms on a cold-moon Vietnam night," O'Brien went to war because he feared "censure, embarrassment, the end of everything that had happened in my life, the end of it all."[2] Likewise, the protagonist of O'Brien's excellent novel, *Going After Cacciato*, goes to war knowing that "the moral climate was imperfect." Pfc. Paul Berlin overcomes his moral objections, as he says at one point in the novel, out of "the dread of abandoning all that I hold dear. I am afraid of running away. I am afraid of exile."[3]

However, Philip Caputo's *A Rumor of War* provides the most detailed dismissal of the many moral objections to the war. Writing about his own experience in Vietnam, Caputo admits that he and the other Americans lost their "humanity" in an inhuman war, but then asks, "who was to speak of rules and ethics in a war that had none?"[4] Caputo argues that "everything rotted and corroded quickly over there: bodies, boot leather, canvas, metal, morals" (p.229). For "twenty years of terrorism and fratricide had obliterated most reference points from the country's moral map long before we arrived" (p.xvi); Caputo thereby rationalizes what he refers to as the "brutish state" into which he and his fellow soldiers sank. By blaming the Vietnamese and their debauched moral landscape, Caputo conveniently denies his own responsibility for the brutality he admits participating in.

Caputo's specious logic can best be seen in the final section of his narrative, appropriately entitled "In Death's Grey Land." There Caputo describes an incident that occurred late in his tour of duty, for which he and two others were brought before a court-martial. As a first lieutenant, Caputo ordered two men to go into a village at night and "get" two suspected Viet Cong. Caputo recalls his instructions as : "*you get those goddamn V.C. Snatch 'em up and bring 'em back here, but if they give you any problem, kill 'em*" (p.317). Following his instructions, Caputo's men kill the two suspects, who turn out not to be Viet Cong after all, and the three Americans find themselves facing court-martial on charges that Caputo labels "absurd." In his response to those charges, Caputo again attempts to justify his own conduct, this time by blaming the war itself:

> The deaths of Le Dung and Le Du could not be divorced from the
> nature and conduct of the war. They were an inevitable product
> of the war. As I had come to see it, America could not intervene in
> a people's war without killing some of the people. But to raise
> these points in explanation or extenuation would be to raise a host
> of ambiguous moral questions. It could even raise the question of
> the morality of American intervention in Vietnam [p.323].

The killings were "inevitable," Caputo argues. Thus he exempts himself
from moral responsibility, as if an immoral war excuses immoral individual conduct. But if individuals cannot be held accountable for their
own actions, then who can? Caputo never answers this question.

In effect, *A Rumor of War* denies the very possibility of moral
responsibility, as Zalin Grant argues in "Vietnam as Fable": Caputo
"pleaded that the insanity of the war ... made him do it, and the critics
generously agreed."[5] Caputo fails to take into account that sense of the
other on which morality depends. An activity, not a sentiment, morality
results from an imaginative and sympathetic identification with the
other. By his own account, Caputo fails to achieve this. If taken
seriously, his reasoning would explain away not only his own "incident
at Giao-Tri," but by extension My Lai and every other atrocity committed on both sides of the war. To be sure, the military and the "political
witch doctors like John F. Kennedy" (Caputo's phrase) should be held
morally responsible for the abyss of Vietnam. Beyond a doubt, the
policies of government and military officials led to the repeated
atrocities that plagued the war, as Caputo alleges. But those who actually
carried out the executions of the women and children at My Lai, for
example, certainly share that moral responsibility. To argue otherwise is
sheer sophistry.

In contrast to *A Rumor of War*, two Vietnam novels do confront
this question of moral responsibility: Victor Kolpacoff's *The Prisoners of
Quai Dong* (1967) and Robert Stone's *Dog Soldiers* (1974). A military
stockade at Quai Dong provides the setting for Kolpacoff's novel,
narrated by a character named Kreuger, an American ex-lieutenant imprisoned for disobeying a direct order to fire on Viet Cong soldiers. One
day a young Vietnamese prisoner arrives at the stockade, and Kreuger
finds himself summoned to an old tool shed surrounded by barbed wire
and armed guards. Kreuger immediately realizes that he has been called
to participate in the "interrogation" of the prisoner — interrogation
meaning torture. And as the guards seal off the dark Quonset hut and
night begins to fall, Kreuger feels "the uneasy certainty that something
unreasonable was going to happen."[6] Fearing the events to come,
Kreuger cowers in the corner of the room, with a bare light bulb dangling

over his head. *The Prisoners of Quai Dong* chronicles the long night of torture that entraps all of them, captors and captive alike.

Kolpacoff uses the dark room as a transparent metaphor for Vietnam. "Something corrupting was happening to us — not just to the men in the stockade, but to all of us" (p.28), Kreuger realizes. For once inside the room, "to do anything was to incur guilt" (p.81). Once the Vietnamese interrogator by the name of Nguyen begins the torture, the action proceeds like a "Greek drama," Joseph Tetlow writes. Tetlow points out that "as the American and Vietnamese interrogators move inexorably toward violence, the actions seem to be pulled by the Fates from the substance of the actors."[7]

Observing the drama, Kreuger understands that whatever happens he will be as guilty as Lieutenant Buckley or Sergeant McGruder, both of whom have ulterior motives for extracting information from the prisoner — the opportunist Buckley wants the promotion that success will bring, and the sadistic McGruder wants the pleasure of beating the man to death. Very quickly they degenerate into bestiality, Nguyen repeatedly jabbing a knife into the prisoner's abdomen and McGruder beating him mercilessly. "Can't you see what's happening?" (p.110) Kreuger asks, but no one listens. By nightfall the "walls had contracted into a low-ceilinged box with three bare sides of corrugated metal, surrounding us with vertical bands of light and dark, like prison bars" (p.79). They had all become prisoners of Quai Dong.

Later Kreuger learns why he has been included in the proceedings: only he can replace Nguyen, because only he can speak Vietnamese. But another more insidious reason occurs to him as Lieutenant Buckley brings more men into the shed: "slowly I saw that the more of us who shared the responsibility for whatever it was that they wanted to do in that room, the less any of us could be held accountable for later when the reckoning came to be made. There could be no talk of guilt if everyone was an accomplice" (p.90). Such military logic proves identical to Caputo's reasoning in *A Rumor of War*: if everyone is guilty, no one is.

Kolpacoff, however, demonstrates the falsity of that argument through the experience of his narrator. Unlike Caputo, Kolpacoff understands that "the simplest act of watching made [Kreuger] a part of it. Even if you did not struggle on either side, you sank into the guilt of it, like quicksand" (p.170). And when Kreuger acts, ostensibly to help the young prisoner, he only contributes to the horror of the proceedings. For example, replacing Nguyen and assuming the "role of the Inquisitor" so as to not hand the boy over to McGruder, Kreuger too ends up using the knife. To finally stop the torture, he deceives Buckley by telling him that the prisoner mentioned the village of Bien Thieu, implying that more Viet Cong can be found there. Kreuger thinks he has ended the ordeal and saved the boy's life, but he discovers his error in the morning when Buckley sends out a squadron of helicopters to attack the unfortunate village. The helicopters, Kreuger learns, "flattened the place with rockets" —a "turkey shoot" (p.209), McGruder boasts. Thus not only does Kreuger share the guilt of the "Inquisitor," but he must assume personal responsibility for the deaths of countless civilians in Bien Thieu. And when the prisoner takes his own life through Kreuger's negligence, the tragedy concludes, the circle of guilt complete. Ironically, the novel ends with Kreuger's reinstatement to rank for his part in the successful interrogation.

But the ironic ending does not lessen the impact of Kolpacoff's novel. Whoever enters the dark room, whoever enters Vietnam, sinks into the quagmire of guilt. Kolpacoff reverses Caputo's expedient logic, and his fiction demonstrates the collective guilt, the moral responsibility of all the Inquisitors. Whether one participates in or merely observes (or even tries to stop) the Inquisition makes no difference: everyone is guilty of everything. To avoid guilt, one must not enter Vietnam; and to avoid further guilt, one must get out as quickly as possible. Otherwise, "escape was impossible," Kreuger realizes.

Robert Stone's *Dog Soldiers* also argues eloquently for collective moral responsibility. The National Book Award winning novel provides brilliant insights into the impact of the Vietnam War on an already disintegrating American culture. Though roughly only a third of its action takes place in Vietnam, the book overflows with violence. Apocalyptic warnings occur throughout the novel, and a sense of doom haunts Stone's dissipated characters as they proceed blindly into the "big shit storm" coming toward them. "Time's short," a strange missionary character says near the beginning, "we're in the last days now."[8] To which Converse, Stone's protagonist, responds: "God in the whirlwind" (p.7), referring to Job 37.

Later in the novel Converse says, "they say the world is coming to an end. They say that's why it's so fucked up" (p.332). As the "secular world" explodes into violence, and the spiritual world expires in exhaustion, Converse and the other characters find themselves in a "world breaking down into degeneracy and murder" (p.274). Vietnam provides Stone with a perfect metaphor for the modern world, in which man cohabits with violence and death, lost on the brink of annihilation. And more, Vietnam becomes that place where modern man (specifically, modern American man) discovers his dissolute condition—"the place where everybody finds out who they are" (p.56), Converse says. America has looked into the mirror of the war and seen the ugly truth about itself—the brutality that, once unleashed, mushrooms into fantasies of total destruction. "You can't blame us too much," Converse says. "We didn't know who we were till we got here. We thought we were something else" (p.57).

Converse comes to Vietnam as a "journalist of sorts," mostly to escape the sleazy porno newspaper he works for back in San Francisco. Faced with the horror of Vietnam, Converse finds himself paralyzed with fear—"the world's most frightened man" (p.11), another character refers to him as. His name itself suggests contradiction or antithesis, an inversion of human values. For in Vietnam Converse loses what little moral perspective he had, and as a consequence he experiences a "difficulty in responding to moral objections" (p.40). For example, when he witnesses a terrorist bombing in downtown Saigon that bears unmistakable resemblance to the street bombing in *The Quiet American*, Converse feels only "numb" and "stupid." Unlike Fowler, Greene's narrator, Converse's observation of the random killing does not prompt him to take a moral stand on the war. In fact, Converse "could not even think of a moral. It reminded him of the lizards smashed on his hotel wall" (p.37). Instead, Converse escapes by taking refuge in drugs and alcohol, and by retiring to the lobby of his hotel to watch "Bonanza" on the Armed Forces Television Network. Converse even rationalizes his moral failure by remembering the "Great Elephant Zap," in which United States Army helicopters had exterminated entire herds of elephants because the animals were occasionally used by the Viet Cong to carry supplies: "as for dope, Converse thought, and addicts—if the world is going to contain elephants pursued by flying men, people are just naturally going to want to get high." And "that's the way it's done," Converse decides. "He had confronted a moral objection and overridden it" (p.42).

Converse's moral laxity leads him to become involved in a scheme to smuggle heroin into the States. Having "fallen in" with the smugglers, Converse allows himself to be talked into the mad scheme: because of "his own desperate emptiness ... he was unable to refuse" them (pp.24-25). But his inability to refuse has enormous consequences that Converse does not foresee, for he involves both his old friend Hicks and his wife Marge in the scheme—Hicks to carry the heroin to San Francisco and Marge to sell it to the "connection." Unfortunately, the connection turns out to be two federal agents who attempt to take the dope without paying for it, and a violent struggle ensues. Hicks and Marge abscond with the drugs, hiding out in the decadent environs of Los Angeles and trying to sell the hot merchandise, pursued by the two agents and their Machiavellian superior, Antheil. The novel's suspenseful plot follows the characters on a trail of death and destruction that ends in a crescendo of violence. Thus Converse's "desperate emptiness," his inability to refuse, leads inexorably to mayhem and murder.

But *Dog Soldiers* proves a much more complicated work of fiction than its plot would indicate, in that Stone (like Kolpacoff) has written a very subtle allegory of the Vietnam War. With his moral turpitude and cowardice, Converse represents all those Americans who refused to take a stand on the war, allowing the war to happen. A "feckless and disorderly person," Converse repeatedly finds himself "at the mercy of events" (p.182), unable to stop the chain of events that his own weakness has initiated. As Stone makes clear, Converse bears personal responsibility for the tragedy that ensues, including the death of Hicks and the addiction of Marge to the fugitive heroin. For her part, Marge shares Converse's "desperate emptiness," and like Converse she finds herself unable to refuse the drug deal. She embraces the scam just as so many Americans embraced the war: out of spiritual exhaustion, moral impoverishment. Unlike Converse, Marge does not even need to overcome "moral objections" because she has none to overcome, only a perverse emptiness that the drug caper temporarily fills.

Ironically, Marge becomes addicted to the heroin, a casualty of the "caper," just as so many Americans became casualties of the war. And in the end, Marge embraces a total nihilism: "if I could pray ... I would pray that God would cause the bomb to fall on all of us." "That's that answer," she says, "the final solution" (p.231). Marge's death wish, her "cheap junkie pessimism," reflects the disillusionment so many Americans felt in the aftermath of the Vietnam War.

Hicks, too, plays a part in Stone's allegory. A former "professional Marine" who thinks of himself as a "kind of Samurai," Hicks can be seen as representative of the American military in Vietnam. Not only does Hicks take pride in his own virility, he believes in his ability to "manipulate matter in a simple disciplined manner, to move things correctly" (p.76) — the very illusion that led the American military deeper and deeper into Vietnam. Inhabiting a "world of objects," Hicks considers human life as matter to be manipulated by the strong. "We're everybody's meat" (p.110), he says to Marge at one point in the novel, referring to humanity in general. Once Hicks accepts the challenge of running drugs, his machismo will not permit him to surrender the bags of heroin, for that would be to admit his own impotence. Appropriately armed with an M-16 rifle and an M-70 grenade launcher, Hicks leads the pursuing federal agents into a desert wilderness a few miles from the Mexican border — a journey as doomed as United States involvement in Vietnam. There, Hicks makes his last stand on top of a mountain, a last stand that Stone likens to a "battle," to "Dienbienphu." A minor character by the name of Dieter describes Hicks perfectly: "he's trapped in a Samurai fantasy — an American one. He has to be the Lone Ranger, the great desperado — he has to win all the epic battles single-handed" (p.272). But Hicks does not win this battle; he only succeeds in getting himself and several other people killed in the carnage that concludes the novel. The federal agents get the heroin, and Hicks dies from his wounds while walking down a railroad track to nowhere, with the useless M-16 slung over his shoulder.

Pearl K. Bell has pointed out another important symbol in *Dog Soldiers.* In "Writing About Vietnam," Bell argues that Stone makes use of the "heroin traffic between Vietnam and the U.S. as an ominous symbol of the creeping moral attrition licensed by a war of attrition."[9] Heroin becomes a symbol of the debilitating effect of Vietnam on our national consciousness, culminating finally in the apathy of the Watergate years. Just as heroin poisons the lives of Converse and the other characters, Vietnam poisoned a generation of Americans and produced a profound cynicism about government and politics in general. And in the allegory of *Dog Soldiers,* the war was fought and all the lives were lost for an illegal stash of narcotics—not even Pound's "an old bitch gone in the teeth" given up "For a botched civilization," but death for two bags of white powder.

Both Stone and Kolpacoff portray Vietnam in remarkably similar metaphors. In *Dog Soldiers* Vietnam becomes a dark retributive presence that infects an entire culture, and in *The Prisoners of Quai Dong* it becomes a dark prison in which "to do anything was to incur guilt." The two novelists agree on how deeply the war enervated our culture, and on the need to confront the moral responsibility that we all share for what happened in Vietnam. Peter Marin makes this very argument in an article in *Harper's* entitled "Coming to Terms with Vietnam." Marin writes that we all "are responsible for the acts of war, accountable for the personal and social acts that contribute to war long before it has begun: the distractions, evasions, failures of nerve and resistance, mindless enthusiasms and neutralities with which we replace our responsibilities as citizens, as moral agents." As moral agents, "we must concern ourselves with the discovery of fact, the location of responsibility, the discussion of causes, the acknowledgment of moral debt and how it might be repaid—not in terms of who supposedly led us astray, but in terms of how each one of us may have contributed to the war or to its underlying causes."[10] Only by acknowledging how we all contributed to the war, can we ever hope to come to terms with Vietnam.

Dog Soldiers and *The Prisoners of Quai Dong* clearly demonstrate the danger of allowing a feeling of powerlessness to excuse moral irresponsibility. Stone, especially, creates characters who, stripped of "moral objections," descend into bestiality. Converse, for example, while caught in an air raid, sees man as moving "heedless and half-assed toward nonentity" (p.185). Unable to affirm human values, Converse concludes by reducing man to the level of "living dogs" who lived, not for any purpose, but because living "was all they knew." To escape this fate, man must engage in what Stone refers to as "moral explorations in the face of mass murder and young oblivion" (p.262).

Chapter 9. Casualties

The Pepsi Generation. Throwaway People

> The ultimate in throwaway people.
> That's what we are. The ultimate
> luxury of a throwaway society. —
> Charles Durden, *No Bugles, No Drums.*

The literature of the Vietnam War reads in spirit like a mere catalogue of the dead. To call roll, to remember all the casualties of a war many people do not wish to remember, becomes the overriding purpose of much of this literature. Like the Marine whose words are recorded in Herr's *Dispatches*: "Okay, man, you go on out of here you cocksucker, but I mean it, you tell it! You tell it, man. If you don't tell it...."[1] Or Caputo's tribute to a fallen comrade in *A Rumor of War*: "As I write this, eleven years after your death, the country for which you died wishes to forget the war in which you died. Its very name is a curse."[2] Herr,

70

Caputo, and many others provide literary testimonials to all the lost friends, all the lost brothers and husbands, sons and fathers. And these writers document other losses as well, losses even greater in a cultural sense: the lost idealism of the Kennedy era, and the lost faith in Johnson's Great Society. Together, the Vietnam books constitute a literature of loss, telling the stories of a generation of Americans used and thrown away in the jungles of Vietnam.

As Mark Baker writes in his recent *Nam*, a generation of Americans were "wasted" in Vietnam. And "when they returned home, they were wasted again, like greasy paper plates after the picnic." They were "disposable soldiers," Baker concludes, "men and women who were treated like so much human refuse to be lugged to the dump."[3] *Nam* and Al Santoli's *Everything We Had*, both oral histories of the war as told by Vietnam veterans and both published in 1981, offer recent portraits of these "disposable soldiers." Earlier, Robert Jay Lifton provided a very moving account of Vietnam veterans in his *Home from the War* (1973), and Gloria Emerson recorded the enormous suffering of both Americans and Vietnamese in her *Winners and Losers* (1976) — a book in which there are no winners, only losers. Even earlier, Ronald J. Glasser related his experience working as a doctor in a United States Army hospital in Japan in his *365 Days* (1971). Treating from 6,000 to 8,000 casualties of the war each month, Glasser described the "victims" as being "written off each month — a wastage rate — a series of contrapuntal numbers, which seems to make it all not only acceptable, but strangely palatable as well."[4] And in *Friendly Fire* (1976), C.D.B. Bryan documented the story of the Millen family and their radicalization after the death of their son in Vietnam. The Millen's loss, one of some 57,000 such losses, became representative of all the nation's losses. For "they, like their son, like the nation itself, had become casualties of the war," Bryan writes.[5]

Not surprisingly, much Vietnam literature depicts the veterans as "human refuse," exploited and then tossed aside by their own society. Exploited, first of all, in the sense that the veterans were sent off to fight someone else's war, only to return to the indifference of their own government and the contempt of many of their own countrymen. Coming home to the same hostility they had experienced in Vietnam, the veterans' transition from military to civilian life proved difficult, like going "from a free-fire zone to the twilight zone," one veteran remarks in *Nam*.[6] However, these books suggest a second, even more sinister form of exploitation, an exploitation rooted deep in an economic system that reduces human life to a commodity. Not simply capitalism, but *advanced consumer capitalism* and its organization of consumption as well as production, comes under fire repeatedly in this literature. For advanced consumer capitalism has created what Charles Durden refers to in *No*

Bugles, No Drums as a "throwaway society," in which human life has been reduced to the status of consumer goods to be purchased, expended, and discarded. This systematic, institutional exploitation results in the phenomenon of "throwaway people," perfectly illustrated by the veterans who were "shipped off to the Army by an IBM machine" and "kept fighting a war nowhere so there will not be a revolution somewhere," as Eastlake writes in *The Bamboo Bed*.[7]

Ron Kovic tells the story of his own exploitation in *Born on the Fourth of July* (1976). Wounded in Vietnam and crippled from the chest down, Kovic returns home only to be shuffled from one incompetent Veterans Administration hospital to another, each of which he likens to a "prison" or a "concentration camp." The inadequate and inhumane treatment he receives at these institutions radicalizes him: "I have been lying in room 17 for almost a month. I am isolated here because I am a troublemaker. I had a fight with the head nurse of the ward. I asked for a bath. I asked for the vomit to be wiped from the floor. I asked to be treated like a human being."[8] After his release, Kovic joins the Vietnam Veterans Against the War and begins to speak out publicly against the war. "I'm the example of the war," he tells his audiences: "Yes, let them get a look at me. Let them be reminded of what they'd done when they'd sent my generation off to war" (p.136).

Not until much later in the narrative does Kovic learn to recognize his true "enemies." While picketing President Nixon's campaign headquarters in 1972, Kovic gets beaten up and arrested by undercover agents, and at that moment he understands just how he and his fellow veterans have been used. He had been their "Yankee Doodle Dandy" and their "all-American boy," and now "they weren't satisfied with three-quarters being gone, they wanted to take the rest of him." For he "had never been anything but a thing to them, a thing to put a uniform on and train to kill, a young thing to run through the meat-grinder, a cheap small nothing thing to make mincemeat out of" (pp.151-52).

In his outrage and his humiliation at being beaten and jailed, Kovic does not quit as he knows "they" want him to. Instead, he becomes even more involved in the campaign to stop the war, for he knows that he has "the power to make people remember, to make them as angry as he was every day of his life, every moment of his existence" (p.153). Recognizing this power, he and his colleagues organize the Last Patrol, which descends on the Republican National Convention in Miami that August. From all over the country they come "to tell Nixon a thing or two. We know we are fighting the real enemies this time — the ones who have made profit off our very lives" (p.158). Kovic describes his "real enemies" as "small men with small ideas, gamblers and hustlers who had gambled with his life and hustled him off to the war. They were smooth talkers, men who wore suits and smiled and were polite, men who wore watches and sat behind big desks sticking pins in maps in rooms he had never seen, men who had longwinded telephone conversations and went home to their wives and children" (p.152). Government, military, and corporate executives, these men profit from the losses of others.

The Republican National Convention concludes Kovic's narrative. Kovic manages to sneak into the convention hall and to get interviewed by Roger Mudd of CBS News. Live on national television, Kovic says "I'm a Vietnam veteran. I gave America my all and the leaders of this government threw me and the others away to rot in their V.A. hospitals. What's happening in Vietnam is a crime against humanity" (p.165). And later as Nixon gives his acceptance speech, Kovic and another veteran disrupt the speech and shout down the President. "This was the moment I had come three thousand miles for," Kovic writes, "this was it, all the pain and the rage, all the trials and the death of the war and what had been done to me and a generation of Americans by all the men who had lied to us and tricked us, by the man who stood before us in the convention hall that night, while men who had fought for their country were being gassed and beaten in the streets outside the hall" (p.168). Shouting down the President, sitting in front of the cameras for all the world to see, becomes Kovic's symbolic triumph, however small — an appropriate conclusion to a memoir written, as Kovic says earlier, to make people remember what he remembers every day of his life.

Because of its personal nature, *Born on the Fourth of July* remains the most moving portrait of disposable soldiers. However, two of the more ambitious Vietnam novels, Durden's *No Bugles, No Drums* (1976) and Stone's *Dog Soldiers* (1974), examine the throwaway society in more detail. Pfc. Jamie Hawkins narrates his own story in *No Bugles, No Drums*, a story of his growing disillusionment with the war and those who control and profit by it. Part of the "Pepsi Generation," Hawkins has been brainwashed by his consumer society and overwhelmed by the media, old movies on TV, and mindless bravado of official propagandists who entice young men into the dark jungles of Vietnam, where they die "for some stupid reason like honor where there ain't none."[9] Hawkins and his generation have all been sold a bill of goods, false notions of honor and patriotism that are packaged and marketed like any other consumer item. They had all been raised on late night television movies, movies that, as Hawkins says, "have done more to make romantic bullshit outa bad business than any single industry ever known" (pp.85-86). The war itself, exported to Southeast Asia like Alden Pyle's Buick in *The Quiet American*, becomes a kind of deadly merchandise: "Fuck the French, it's Americans who gave us Fords, frozen food 'n' free-fire zones. Mass production, goopy strawberries 'n' legal murder" (p.177-78).

Here Durden, through his fictional observer, touches on a crucially important concept: war as commodity in advanced consumer capitalism. No ironic distance exists between Durden and his narrator, and Hawkins obviously speaks for Durden when he equates "Fords" and "free-fire zones," "mass production" and "legal murder." By such equations, Durden implies that the war is a function of advanced consumer capitalism. Like so much merchandise, the war was mass-marketed and sold to a consumer society conditioned to consume the latest fashions, whether automobiles or wars. Even more important, the war provided promotions, profits and power for those who orchestrated it. Though the war might have been "bad," business was good.

This theory can be supported by examining the ever-shifting and at times contradictory reasons for fighting the war. In fact, Vietnam was notable for an absence of ideology, as the fervor to contain communism quickly gave way to more pragmatic reasons for remaining in Indochina, reasons that changed with and mirrored the worsening political and military situation in South Vietnam. To fulfill our SEATO obligations, to protect our national security, to support our ally, and finally to save face, all blurred together after so many years and so many losses. This confusion appears most clearly in the testimony of those men sent to fight the war, in their stories and their attempts to sift through the incoherent reasons for the war and to find something to believe in, something to fight for. Durden portrays and Hawkins experiences such a war in *No Bugles, No Drums*: a war fought not for ideology, but for economics.

Hawkins very quickly realizes the truth about this consumer war. After his first battle, which leaves 17 of his comrades dead, he feels blank, empty. "I couldn't think of anything," he says. "Not a fuckin' thing. The first verse of 'Flanders Field' came to mind. And that Pepsi ad... *You've got a lot to live, and Pepsi's got a lot to give.* Maybe that's the thing, the epitaph, I guess it's called, for this war" (p.23). Hawkins realizes here that the war is as pointless and jingoistic as the Pepsi ad and most other consumer items, sold as they are by means of catchy phrases and extensive public relations campaigns. Hawkins also becomes class conscious, discovering that most of his fellow soldiers are poor, lower-class kids like himself. Blacks and other minorities serve as "cannon fodder," while white middleclass officers obsessed with promotion play sophisticated and deadly versions of cowboys and Indians. As one black character remarks, "they finally figured a way to kill spades 'n' slopes at the same time" (p.123). Hawkins and the others have been "pulled from the compost heap of America's hopeless" and recycled to Vietnam, fuel to be consumed by their consumer society so that the "right people" may exercise their power and their profit. "The Ultimate in throwaway people," Hawkins calls them, calls himself. "That's what we are. The ultimate luxury of a throwaway society" (p.166).

The "right people," as Hawkins defines them, include both high-ranking officials of the military-industrial complex, and all the other "fuckin' thieves, war profiteers, black-market motherfuckers, the ego-centered bigoted bastards lookin' to get promoted" (p.210). For their benefit, he and the others spend their time in Vietnam pursuing the elusive Viet Cong on relentless patrols, waiting for sudden death on narrow jungle trails. They live and die not to win the war, which they know is impossible, but to produce high body counts in order to make their colonel look good. Hawkins grows bitter and disillusioned, and the novel comes to a brutal conclusion in a fatal last patrol. After Hawkins' platoon has been overrun by Viet Cong, the colonel gets his high body count by calling in long-range artillery and killing Viet Cong and Americans alike. Only Hawkins survives, and he carries the decapitated body of his lieutenant back to battalion headquarters, presenting the grisly corpse as an offering to the colonel. Hawkins' only victory, if it can be called a victory, lies in the success of the madness he feigns thereupon, which allows him to be discharged early. Permanently disillusioned, left only with his "bad attitude," Hawkins has been thrown away just as effectively as his dead comrades. He can only say, finally: "Fuck his country, my country, your country. It sucks. Political pigs, corporate dictators..." (p.210).

In *Dog Soldiers* Robert Stone provides even a more ominous portrait of those who control the throwaway society. Like Hawkins in *No Bugles, No Drums*, Stone's three main characters (Converse, his wife Marge, and his friend Hicks) all belong to the class of throwaway people. While working as a journalist in Vietnam, Converse gets involved in a scheme to smuggle heroin into the States; he discovers too late that his connection in Saigon works with a federal regulatory agent by the name of Antheil back in San Francisco. Antheil's position of authority allows him to commandeer hard drugs and sell them himself, from the inside. When Antheil attempts to take this particular shipment of heroin by force, Marge and Hicks resist and make the fatal mistake of fleeing, unaware of Antheil's power and connections. In the ensuing pursuit, Antheil and his henchmen become the hunters, and Marge and Hicks, and later Converse, become the hunted. As Hicks says to Marge at one point in the novel: "we're everybody's meat."[10]

Stone uses the heroin traffic between Vietnam and the States as a symbol of the moral attrition caused by the Vietnam War. Though the drug traffic, and by extension the war, poisons the moral life of an entire culture, it also provides enormous profits for Antheil and those like him. Stone succeeds in making both Charmian, who organizes the drug scheme in Saigon, and Antheil representative of the power-brokers who control their society. Charmian, for example, has influential political "connections"—her father had been a judge in Florida, and at one time she had been the mistress of a powerful "influence peddler" and "wheeler-dealer" in Washington. Later she had worked for the United States Information Agency and for an Atlanta-based broadcasting syndicate. Decadent and opportunistic, she belongs to a kind of international diplomatic jet set, occasionally flying over to Phnom Penh to "get stoned and have a massage" (p.16). She likes Saigon, Stone writes with a touch of sarcasm, because "it was a bit like Washington." The dope is plentiful, and business is good.

As her name suggests, Charmian acts the part of an enchantress—she employs her carnality, as well as her political connections, to get what she wants. Antheil is a much more frightening character, as ruthless as he is greedy and corrupt. Like Charmian, Antheil "knows a lot of heavy political people": "he's got a lot of sources. He pays them" (p.180), one of his henchmen says. A lawyer as well as a federal regulatory agent, Antheil has also worked for the Civil Service Commission and the Internal Revenue. Significantly, his name resembles the German word *Anteil*, which means "share," "portion," or "interest." In other words, Antheil symbolizes the acquisitive or predatory economic system he serves and personifies—captitalism. Antheil *is* the "system," and he sums up his philosophy when he says in a passage that concludes the novel: "if you think someone's doing you wrong, it's not for you to judge. Kill them first and then God can do the judging" (p.342).

Dog Soldiers comes to an extremely dark conclusion, like *No Bugles, No Drums*. After torturing Converse and killing Hicks, Antheil and his thugs manage to take possession of the heroin. Converse and Marge survive, as does Hawkins in *No Bugles, No Drums*, but they too have become casualties—their lives shattered, Marge addicted to the heroin. They survive, but only because Antheil chooses not to dispose of them. To Antheil, Converse and his wife count as no more than an "itch" or a "sore" to be eliminated whenever it suits his purpose. Hicks speaks for all the throwaway people when he says "we're everybody's meat": "two hundred million rat-hearted cocksuckers in enormous cars. Rabbits and fish" (p.325). Rabbits and fish to be eaten by those like Antheil, little people who together form a "chain of victims"—this becomes Robert Stone's vision of America in *Dog Soldiers*, his own version of a "throwaway society."

One other Vietnam novel presents a slightly different variation. of this theme. Though not so highly regarded (and rightfully so) as Durden's or Stone's novel, George Davis' *Coming Home* (1971) portrays the imperialism of the Vietnam War as an effort on the part of America to

export its "throwaway society" to Vietnam. After all, the Americans attempted to recreate South Vietnam in their own image: successive Saigon
regimes, like the war itself, were mass-marketed by means of an extensive advertising campaign. To the Americans, the entire population of
South Vietnam became throwaway people, there to be expended like so
much coin in the building of a consumer society, conveniently labelled a
"national democracy" for better public relations.

Interestingly enough, *Coming Home* bears no resemblance what-
soever to the movie of the same name (see Chapter 10). The main characters of the novel happen to be black, a far cry from the glamorized
Hollywood version that starred Jane Fonda and John Voigt. While the
movie capitalized on the sentimental notion of the war as an American
tragedy, the novel focuses on the insensitivity and brutality of the
Americans and their attempt to "save" Vietnam by destroying it. Thus
Davis' main character, a black pilot by the name of Ben, refuses to fly
any more bombing missions because he recognizes the cruelty of his own
countrymen and because he grows tired of "helping white men keep their
hold over the world."[11] Ben, too, has been a victim of racism, both at
home and in Vietnam, where his superiors are all white. Fighting a white
man's war, Ben "can only hate whitey for the smaller symptoms of the
disease that he is spreading around the world, like segregating the whore-
houses and bathhouses over here" (pp.17-18). Ben sees the war as a simple attempt to "enslave" the Vietnamese, and he places the war in the
historical perspective of 19th and 20th century imperialism. White men,
coming to Third World countries, "called them backward or uncivilized.
They hated them and used them and justified whatever they did to them
by invoking some kind of divine right of commerce. Discovered them,
Christianized them, annihilated them or tried to make them into tools —
hoes and cotton-pickers and brooms and shoeshine rags — for the great
march of civilization" (p.119). But by "civilization," as Ben well knows,
the white man means only the "divine right of commerce" — exploitation
for the white man's profit. (In other words, the white man profits by
keeping open and by expanding markets in Third World countries like
Vietnam.) And so Ben deserts at the end of the novel, deciding to live
among the Vietnamese people and leave the Americans to their imperialistic attempt to "safeguard civilization from the Mongolian hordes"
(p.99).

All the works discussed here, both fiction and nonfiction, hold their
political and economic system responsible for the tragedy of Vietnam.
Even more specifically, these books blame government, military, and
corporate executives who sold the war to increase their own power and
profit, and who "wasted" a generation of Americans and millions of Vietnamese by pursuing their own self-interest. These Vietnam books

chronicle the losses of both Americans and Vietnamese, the enormous suffering and the lost lives, the trauma and the disillusionment that remains, undiminished by time. Thus they provide a final tribute to the memory of all the "throwaway people" consumed by a consumer society.

Chapter 10. Derealizing Vietnam: Hollywood

The Celluloid War

> *One, two, three, what are we fightin'*
> *for? Don't ask me; I don't give a damn.*
> *Next stop is Vietnam.* — Country Joe
> and the Fish, "I-feel-like-I'm-fixin'-to-
> die Rag"

Hollywood and Vietnam have had a longstanding if fickle affair. Early Vietnam movies missed the complexities of the war altogether, and when the war became too "controversial" during the 1960s and early 1970s, the film industry shied away from the subject. Later in the decade and in the 1980's, however, Hollywood has turned Vietnam into a major commercial industry, as witnessed by the box-office success of the "big" Vietnam movies — *Coming Home* (1978), *The Deer Hunter* (1979), and *Apocalype Now* (1979). But while profits have been high, truth has been hard to come by in these films. With a few exceptions, most notably *Hearts and Minds* (1975), the Vietnam movies distort the war in many of the same ways that so much of the literature does. By and large, Hollywood has derealized the war by packaging and selling a simplistic, sentimental, soap opera version of American in Vietnam.

The movie version of *The Quiet American* (1958), Hollywood's first, and unsuccessful, venture into the subject, provides an extreme example of distortion. Director (and screenwriter) Joseph L. Mankiewicz completely reverses the meaning of Graham Greene's novel, and in doing so he neuters the English novelist's attack on American involvement in Vietnam. Alden Pyle, the quiet American, played by Audie Murphy, turns out to be the "good guy" — just a naive but well-intentioned American trying to spread light and happiness, and a little American pie, to the Third World. In contrast, Fowler (Michael Redgrave), the English journalist, turns out to be the "bad guy" — cynical, spiteful, deceitful. Like some Cold War Judas, Fowler sets up Pyle only to discover too late, after the quiet American's death, that Pyle was not murderously meddling in Vietnamese politics after all, but was simply importing innocent plastic, not material for terrorists' bombs.

In this curious reversal of roles, Fowler becomes the murderer instead of Pyle, and the movie concludes with an overdose of moralizing dialogue in which Fowler, now chastened and enlightened, must grovel for repentance. Thus Mankiewicz's doctored script degenerates into Cold War propaganda at the end, which I suppose can be partly understood by the period in which the film was made. Few directors would make an anti-American, pro-Communist film in the frigid, black-listed 1950s. But this only partly explains the phenomenon, for the myth of the American innocent, betrayed by both friends and enemies alike, persists even in recent Vietnam movies, *The Deer Hunter* being the most obvious example.

The movie version of *The Green Berets* (1968) demonstrates another Hollywood simplification of the war: the cowboys and Indians, good versus evil melodrama. Unlike *The Quiet American*, John Wayne's *The Green Berets* (which he co-directed and starred in) faithfully follows Robin Moore's novel to the bitter end. As one would expect, the movie relies on the same clichés, the same one-dimensional characters, and the same manichean struggle between "the Communists" and the heroic Americans that the book does. One does not expect any substance from a movie like *The Green Berets*, but what is disturbing is that many later, more sophisticated Vietnam films fail to portray the war in any more depth.

Other Vietnam movies cultivate the sentimental notion (or myth) of the war as an American, not a Vietnamese, tragedy. To date a host of films have been released that explore the ill effects of the war on Vietnam veterans, or on American society as a whole. Such pseudo-Vietnam movies include *Taxi Driver* (1976), *Rolling Thunder* (1977), and *Heroes* (1977). Each of these films centers on Vietnam veterans who have been emotionally disturbed by the war, and each concludes in a climactic firefight obviously meant to conjure up images of Vietnam. Even films as popular as *Coming Home* and *The Deer Hunter* create the impression that the war was exclusively an American tragedy. While these films provide valuable documentation of the physical and psychological trauma suffered by Vietnam veterans, they do not even so much as suggest that the Vietnamese might have suffered too. Watching these films one might assume that the Americans fought each other in the jungle of Vietnam.

In addition to the "big" Vietnam films already mentioned, three minor Vietnam movies deserve comment — *The Boys in Company C* (1977), *Tracks* (1977), and *Who'll Stop the Rain* (1978). As the least successful of these films, Sidney Furie's *The Boys in Company C* suffers from a confusion of intention. The movie does, more or less realistically, depict the brutality of the war — the atrocities and the enormous waste of life. However, the film relies too heavily on the contrived convention of the World War II patrol picture, the platoon composed of representatives of every race, color, and creed. Moreover, the movie falls back on a frivolity reminiscent of *M*A*S*H*, which appears to be the only way Furie could extricate himself from his unpleasant subject matter. The film concludes in a wild soccer game that the Americans must manage to loose or they will be sent back to the front. "Given the choice between coming out of the war alive and self-respect," Al Auster and Leonard Quart write, in "Hollywood and Vietnam," "the Americans choose to win and march off whistling. The message is hardly subtle — G.I. Joe is still a winner."[1] While amusing, the scene hardly supplies a resolution to any of the problems the film touches upon earlier.

The low-budget *Tracks*, directed by Henry Jaglom, presents a much more interesting story of the psychological disintegration of one Vietnam veteran. Dennis Hopper gives an excellent performance as a United States Army sergeant who believes himself to be escorting the body of a friend killed in Vietnam back to a hero's hometown burial. On his cross-country train ride, from West to East, the sergeant corners several of the other passengers and tries to tell them about his friend, supposedly a black soldier who had once saved his life. But the other passengers do not want to hear about any of this, especially when the sergeant asks if anyone can explain what exactly Vietnam was *for.* The others react to the sergeant and his question with a mixture of embarrassment, indifference, and occasional hostility. What makes this film so powerful, as

John Pym points out in "A Bullet in the Head: Vietnam Remembered," is the sergeant's "fractured, haunted attempts to come to terms with normality, with people not concerned solely with killing and staying alive, but with picking up girls, chess problems and baseball statistics."[2] The sergeant realizes, finally and painfully, that his fellow passengers (and his fellow Americans, the movie implies) do not give a damn about him or Vietnam, or about his struggle to regain the sense of innocence he feels he lost in Vietnam.

In spite of its many powerful moments, *Tracks* is ultimately flawed because of an unrealistic, heavy-handed ending. Once the coffin reaches its destination and no one turns out for the funeral, the sergeant leaps into the grave and opens the apparently empty coffin. When he emerges, dressed in combat fatigues and armed with full battle gear, he embarks on an improbable assault on the society that produced both him and the war. Alone, he cries out "you want to go to Nam? I'll take you there." The film fails here, at the moment Jaglom attempts to turn his character into a kind of avenging angel who will somehow bring the war "home" to his banal, indifferent countrymen.

Who'll Stop the Rain, directed by Karel Reisz, also fails to live up to its potential. The movie does not do justice to its source, Robert Stone's *Dog Soldiers*. In fact, the film suffers from Reisz's inability or refusal to translate into cinema the various connections that Stone makes (e.g., heroin smuggling as metaphor for the moral attrition licensed by the war, or Vietnam as metaphor for the violence and inhumanity of American society). The ten minutes of war scenes at the beginning of the movie do not suffice to establish Stone's equations, nor do they provide sufficient motivation for the main characters and their obsessive commitment to the heroin scheme. As a consequence, the action seems disconnected, not grounded in the cultural disintegration caused by the Vietnam War. Not even some excellent performances can compensate for this absence of context.

In addition, as other critics have pointed out, Reisz tampers with the conclusion of *Dog Soldiers*. For example, William J. Palmer writes in "The Vietnam War Films" that "with its final image of the heroin blowing in the New Mexico wind," the film becomes "a rock and roll version of *Treasure of the Sierra Madre*."[3] Reisz, incomprehensibly it would seem, turns the last scene into a melodrama of greed, with Antheil down on his hands and knees in a half-comic pose desperately trying to scoop up the white powder, while behind him Angel prepares to shoot him in the back for the fast-disappearing heroin. Thus, disintegrating into a moralistic farce, *Who'll Stop the Rain* irretrievably muddles Stone's portrait of a predatory society, as personified by Antheil and his henchmen, that exploits and disposes its own people for power and profit. Instead of a critique of advanced consumer capitalism, Reisz gives us a platitudinous study of characters locked in a circle of greed.

Though more popular, and technically more sophisticated, the "big" Vietnam movies have their share of problems as well. Critical reaction to *Coming Home*, *The Deer Hunter*, and *Apocalypse Now* has been mixed, to say the least. In fact, the two latter movies have precipitated violent, polemical diatribes from both supporters and detractors. Of the three, *Coming Home* seems to be the safest — that is, the least controversial. To its credit, the film portrays the dilemma of the disabled Vietnam veteran, the newest group of forgotten, invisible Americans. "When people look they don't see me," the paraplegic Luke, played by John Voigt, tells Sally Hyde, played by Jane Fonda. Luke's personal struggle to regain his self-esteem, not to mention some semblance of the normal life he led before the war, makes for all that is good in *Coming Home*. As the movie opens, a group of Vietnam veterans are talking and shooting pool, and one disabled veteran tells another "you got to justify it to yourself, so you say it's okay. If you don't do that the whole thing was a waste." How do we make it okay? how do we come to terms with Vietnam? become the questions posed by the film. Unfortunately, director Hal Ashby cannot finally produce an answer to that crucial question.

Ostensibly about the painful process of healing the wounds of Vietnam, *Coming Home* degenerates into the soap opera love story of Luke and Sally. While husband Bob fights in Vietnam, wife Sally romances with Luke and experiences a titillating sexual metamorphosis: her hair comes down frizzy, her pantsuits give way to Levis, she has wonderfully intense orgasms and, in the meantime, turns against the war. Not a bad scenario for an adult, counterculture fairytale played out against a background of 1960s rock music that, sometimes rather too obviously, comments on the action.

Fonda's sudden liberation has as much depth as her and Voigt's dubbed sex scenes, but the character of Bob, played by Bruce Dern, is even more one-dimensional. Disturbed by his experience in Vietnam, as well as cuckolded by Luke, Bob conveniently turns into a psychotic and disposes of himself by walking naked into the ocean in a scene so unconvincing and melodramatic that it nearly negates all the movie's good qualities. *Coming Home* would have been much better had it not been for what Palmer refers to as the "clumsy, insensitive handling of the character of Bob Hyde"[4] (and the "PVS" or Post Vietnam Syndrome in general).

The problem, then, is that Hal Ashby takes the easy way out. Instead of squarely facing the problems of a nation desperately in need of healing itself after Vietnam, he falls back on the old Hollywood cliché: a love story, with a little oral sex thrown in to bring it up to date. Luke and

Sally, we are led to believe, will live happily ever after — as if that could provide an answer to the thousands of Vietnam veterans still suffering physical and emotional problems from the war, or as if that could regenerate a nation bitterly divided over the moral quandries of Vietnam. Somewhere in the course of the movie, the war becomes secondary to Ms. Fonda's orgasms, and like the character of Bob Hyde, *Coming Home* drowns in a sea of sentiment. As Auster and Quart write, "politically *[Coming Home]* is a liberal, safe film, and, finally, too conventional — too dependent on heavy-handed crosscutting, soft-focus photography and rock music (Voigt's and Fonda's lyrical love scene, with 'Strawberry Fields' on the sound track) to really get to the psychic and political core of Vietnam."[5]

The Deer Hunter, directed by Michael Cimino, cannot be so easily dismissed. In many ways a much more disturbing movie, *The Deer Hunter* elicited angry responses from leftist reviewers who found it racist and distasteful. However, many of these same reviewers admitted the emotional power of the movie, which results from Cimino's relentless portrait of the impact of the war on one small workingclass community in Pennsylvania. Peter Marin, for example, calls Cimino to account for his "intentional misrepresentations of the war, his implicit absolution of Americans for any illegitimate violence and brutality, and a xenophobia and racism as extravagant as anything to be found on the screen since our second-world-war films about the Japanese." And yet, at the same time, Marin adds that "Cimino shows more humanity, more respect and generosity, toward his American characters than one can find ... in either *Coming Home* or *Apocalypse Now*."[6] This mixture of rightwing propaganda and workingclass epic has made *The Deer Hunter* probably the most controversial of all Vietnam movies.

Cimino has publicly stated that he did not intend to make a "Vietnam film" or a "political film." He wanted, he insisted, "to make a film about these kind of people — Middle American steelworkers in a Slovak community. Like most ordinary people, they can be extraordinary in the face of crises. So the war is simply a means of testing their courage and will power."[7] To take this statement seriously one would have to be very foolish, for how could a director make a movie about a subject as emotionally charged as Vietnam and avoid political significance? Even more to the point, how could such a movie conclude with a group of unrepentant Americans singing "God Bless America" and not be political?

For his subject Cimino chooses a tightly-knit, ethnic community in a Pennsylvania steel town by the name of Clairton. Michael (Robert De Niro), Nicky (Christopher Walken), and Steven (John Savage), supposedly representative of this Russian immigrant community, work together at the steel mill, play together at the bar, and in fact do everything together. Three other friends complete their cabal of male friend-ship—Stan (John Cazale), Axel (Chuck Aspegren), and John (George Dzundza). Forming a kind of macho cult, the six friends participate in various male-bonding rituals carried out in the best adolescent tradition. No females are allowed to encroach on their revels, for theirs is a sexless world. A cross between fraternity boys and workingclass heroes, they turn everything into a male ritual: drinking, hunting, miming rock music, drag racing. Cimino would have us believe that these men embody the communal codes and rituals of ethnic American laborers. Thus when the three central characters go off to Vietnam and return irrevocably altered, we are supposed to see the dissolution of working-class America itself.

Composed of three parts, *The Deer Hunter* displays what Palmer has referred to, perhaps overly-complimentarily, as a "metaphorical structure." Repeated metaphors link the three sections and express the film's thematic meaning. The movie opens in fire, Palmer points out, "men walking through a Dante-esque inferno ... of the steel mill." Likewise, the middle section, set in Vietnam, begins with a napalm drop and Michael walking through flames, killing with a flame-thrower. "Before, Hell was simply one's place of employment," Palmer writes. "In section two, the flames are beginning to burn out of control. In the final section, in Saigon, Michael returns to float through a world going up in flames. Come finally to the Seventh Circle, he learns from Nicky the hopelessness of hell, the lostness of a whole new generation."[8] Other metaphors, such as drinking (and in Nicky's case heroin addiction) and gambling, recur throughout the film. For example, in the first section Nicky bets and loses on everything from pool shots to passing trucks. Michael, on the other hand, always wins. Their gambling prepares the viewer for the long, excruciating scenes of Russian roulette, the movie's central metaphor, in sections two and three. In the film's climactic scene with Michael and Nicky sitting across the table from each other and taking turns with the revolver, the outcome remains the same. Michael wins, and Nicky blows out his brains.

The first part of the movie focuses on Clairton, on the six friends and their community. Many of the scenes are detailed, realistic, and convincing. However, Cimino flaws his rendition of a workingclass world when he engages in symbolic overkill. The hunting scene comes to mind as the best example of this exaggeration. Cimino turns the hunt into a Wagner opera, with long panoramic shots of towering, snow-capped mountains (supposedly in Pennsylvania!). One expects to see God appearing to Moses rather than a group of steelworkers drinking Rolling Rock and hunting deer. And when the deer finally appears, the animal looks like something out of Greek mythology with its gigantic antlers (perhaps this is Mount Olympus?). The kill scene, with Michael running through the woods in a too-meticulously staged chase, and with religious choral music booming on the sound track, renders the episode foolish.

However, the hunt scene does accomplish one thing — it provides Cimino with a set-piece with which to develop his characters. Nicky and Steven are both warm and good-natured, Steven rather shy, Nicky rather bumbling. But Cimino dwells on Michael, of whom he is inordinately fond. While the others come to Mount Olympus to drink a few beers and have a good time, Michael takes his hunting and everything else very seriously — deadly seriously. He refuses to loan Stan an extra pair of boots in order to teach his forgetful friend a lesson, and he holds up a single bullet for all to see and declares, in all seriousness, "this is this!"

Michael, it seems, is a one-shot, no-nonsense, hunter-killer who never misses. As such, Michael represents that stereotyped character so familiar in American literature and cinema — the cold, brooding character that D.H. Lawrence referred to as "hard, isolate, stoic, and a killer." Basically a loner, Michael always stands on the periphery of his society, and on the deer hunt he believes that he can test his manhood (in some romantic, psychosexual way) against nature. Michael's friends make fun of his sexual purity; Stan even goes so far as to call him a "faggot." Cimino had the opportunity to explode this shallow, simpleminded stereotype, but instead he celebrated it. For Michael, in spite of his absurdity, remains the leader, the hero, the deer hunter.

Section one concludes in an interesting, if over-extended, wedding sequence. Cimino dwells lavishly on the rituals and ceremonies of the Russian Orthodox Church, once again stressing the ties of ritual and memory that bond his characters to their community. But his love of ceremony does not prevent Cimino from engaging in a little irony. Steven, the bridegroom, must marry because his bride is pregnant, just as all three of the young friends must leave for Vietnam after the wedding. Cimino further makes his point by means of a few, well-chosen omens: a Green Beret who wanders into the adjoining bar and who responds to Michael's greeting with obscenity, and a wedding toast during which three drops of red wine spill onto the bride's dress, indicating bad luck to come. So even in the throes of the wedding ritual, we sense that the little community will soon shatter before our eyes.

And shatter it does, as the next section opens with exploding napalm and Michael firing a flame-thrower. Their adolescent world erupts into violence and death, and the three young heroes almost immediately find themselves prisoners of the Viet Cong, locked in a bamboo cage half-submerged in water and forced to play Russian roulette for the amusement of their captors. Whereas section one stresses community, section two stresses physical and psychological isolation: the characters are alone, trapped like animals. The three of them do finally escape – or rather Michael saves them, actually carrying Steven back to the American lines. Even so, Steven's legs, badly broken, render him a cripple; and Nicky breaks down too, but for a different reason.

In the concluding scene of this section, Nicky wanders into a crowded room in Saigon and discovers two Vietnamese with red head-bands playing a voluntary game of Russian roulette. Men dressed in business suits stand around the players, waving fistfuls of money and betting on the outcome. Then Nicky recognizes Michael among the onlookers, and suddenly his mind snaps (he has only recently been released from the hospital). He rushes forward, seizes the revolver, puts it to his head and pulls the trigger – on an empty chamber. The game breaks up in confusion: Michael watching, and Nicky being escorted out by Julien, the French "fixer" who organizes the spectacles.

In section three Michael returns to Clairton, apparently disoriented and disillusioned. He feels estranged from his friends, and he cannot bring himself to attend a reunion held in his honor. Instead he watches from afar and then takes refuge in a motel, sitting alone and staring out at a dark Pennsylvania river. Even his hunting goes sour, as Michael finds that he cannot pull the trigger on another Mount Olympus deer. "Okay," he yells, and shoots over the animal's head, supposedly implying some new regard for life, or at least a weariness with killing. The only thing Michael has going for him turns out to be Linda, Nicky's girlfriend (played by Meryl Streep). So far so good, but Michael – feeling guilty because he bears some responsibility for Nicky's breakdown, and doubly guilty because he stole his best friend's girl – decides to return to Saigon and bring Nicky home, never mind how.

Michael finds Nicky where he left him, except by now Nicky has become a professional Russian roulette player and is addicted to heroin. Nicky, in fact, fails to recognize Michael until his deer-hunting friend actually buys his way into the game, sits across the table from him, and says "I love you." However, Nicky blows out his brains the very next moment, and Michael must bring his friend's body home to Clairton. Nicky's funeral, or rather a gathering of the remaining friends after the funeral, provides *The Deer Hunter* with its concluding scene. The distraught friends gather in John's Bar and, unable to speak, burst into song: "God Bless America."

This ending, as unexpected as it is shocking, brings into question Cimino's intention, as well as his political consciousness. Does he mean the scene to be ironic, so that everyone might laugh at these people who have never questioned the war or their participation in it, who have no idea who is responsible for their agony and their losses? Or does Cimino intend this scene to be taken seriously, as some kind of reaffirmation or communal healing? I join most critics in taking Cimino seriously here and argue that his too facile attempt at reconciliation seriously flaws the movie. For example, Auster and Quart argue that Cimino falls back, for lack of anything else, on the "American will": "Cimino believes in the power of that will to mute the horror of the war, but one senses here an almost gratuitous leap of faith, an unthinking and self-indulgent embrace of metaphor and ritual."[9]

The Deer Hunter has other problems, as well. For one thing, Cimino's workingclass America, on which the entire edifice of this American tragedy rests, exists only in his imagination. Because of Cimino's superficial treatment, Clairton remains a myth, a cliché lacking any socioeconomic depth. Likewise, Cimino's characters have no more depth than their Pennsylvania steel town; they seem more adolescent than tragic, and they do not, by any means, represent America. Also, Cimino's obsession with Russian roulette as metaphor for United States involvement in Vietnam weakens the film. The metaphor is not only simplistic, but dangerously misleading. However misguided, Americans died in Vietnam for definite political and historical reasons, *not* sitting across a table from each other blowing out their brains for the amusement and/or profit of the Vietnamese. In much the same way that Michael Herr's *Dispatches* reduces Vietnam to "dope and dementia," Cimino's ill-chosen metaphor implies that Vietnam was only a fatal game: random, meaningless, nihilistic.

Even more seriously, Cimino's racism completely distorts what happened in Vietnam. Americans made war on the Vietnamese, not the other way around. Cimino reverses this so that he may create his smug, self-pitying version of Vietnam as an American tragedy. In *The Deer Hunter*, Peter Marin writes, "innocent Americans become the war's only victims, and the Vietnamese – in reality an agrarian, village people – become the big-city villains, smiling devils, corrupt gamblers, street-wise pimps and whores."[10] Cimino's whitewash of American responsibility for Vietnam makes his film very political indeed – as politically reactionary as any book or film made about the Vietnam War.

Though not as self-pitying or as politically claustrophobic, *Apocalypse Now* also suffers from major problems. The movie's release in 1979 became a public "happening" because of massive prerelease publicity – reports of all the years and all the disasters (including Martin Sheen's heart attack) that occurred during the filming, and the reported $30 to $50 million production cost. After its release, *Apocalypse Now* quickly became the most written about movie of recent years. Reviews were mixed, however; most critics praised the early realistic scenes, denounced the last surrealistic third of the film, and objected to director

Francis Ford Coppola's over-reliance on Conrad's *Heart of Darkness.* Peter Marin criticized the entire movie for being "morally stupid ... [and] an essentially unintelligent investigation of themes too complex for Coppola to handle."[11] The debate has even spilled over into the academic journals with the publication of Ronald L. Bogue's defense of the movie, "The Heartless Darkness of *Apocalypse Now*," in a recent issue of the *Georgia Review.* Bogue's essay seems likely to provoke yet more re-evaluation of "Coppola's folly," as some writers have referred to the film.

Unfortunately, detractors of *Apocalypse Now* often overlook the brilliance of the first two-thirds of the movie. Despite its shortcomings, *Apocalypse Now* provides the most powerful cinematic portrait of the war to date. The few brief war scenes in *The Deer Hunter* seem impressionistic and unconvincing by comparison. For perhaps the first time on film, Coppola captures the horror of modern technological warfare. In one memorable scene, an American patrol intercepts a Vietnamese boat and massacres every Vietnamese on board. The Americans begin shooting, not because they are savages or murderers, but because they become paranoid while searching the boat, unable to tell "friendlies" from Viet Cong. That one incident offers more insight into what happened in Vietnam, into why the Americans reacted the way they did, than all other narrative Vietnam movies combined. And of all these films, only *Apocalypse Now* portrays the effects of the war on the Vietnamese people.

In his defense of *Apocalypse Now*, Bogue argues that Coppola's reliance on Conrad's *Heart of Darkness* does not flaw the movie, as many critics have contended. The movie should be seen as an "imitation" rather than an adaption, Bogue maintains. Bogue sees the imitation as "constantly duplicating, displacing, correcting, and contradicting a latent text." Furthermore, the imitation provides a "means of interrogating one's culture by juxtaposing it with an earlier culture."[12] Thus by juxtaposing the American attempt to control Vietnam with the account of 19th century imperialism in *Heart of Darkness*, Coppola criticizes contemporary American culture and exposes its "heartless darkness" (Bogue's term). However, by itself Bogue's semantic distinction does not answer the crucial questions: does Coppola significantly alter (or comment ironically on) Conrad's text? And if so, to what purpose?

Coppola follows *Heart of Darkness* faithfully. He borrows characters and plot, actual bits of dialogue, and many specific details. His narrator, like Conrad's, journeys up a dark river to find the mysterious Kurtz. Conrad's Marlow works for a Belgian trading company, which sends him to bring under control a renegade agent who has succumbed to greed and become a human god worshipped by a primitive tribe in the Congo. Coppola's Marlow, Captain Willard, works as an assassin for the

United States Army, which orders him to "terminate the command" of a renegade Special Forces officer who has organized a private army of Montagnard tribesmen and American deserters in Cambodia. Conrad's Kurtz has become obsessed with ivory, and Coppola's with the "moral terror" of war, and the implied comparison of 19th century imperialism and the Vietnam War is obvious. In fact, both sets of characters work for organizations engaged in "a struggle to subdue recalcitrant natives and establish a lucrative colony," Bogue points out.[13] Thus Colonel Kurtz tells Willard not to think of himself as a soldier, but as "an errand boy for grocery clerks come to collect the price."

But colonialism has changed from the 19th to the 20th century, and the Belgian exploitation of the Congo differs from the American exploitation of Vietnam. The Belgians can still justify their presence in the Congo by invoking idealistic notions of progress and civilization. Kurtz, for example, goes to Africa to manage an ivory trading company as "a beacon on the road towards better things, a center for trade of course, but also for humanizing, improving, instructing." Even Marlow, who has seen the ugly work of imperialism firsthand, and who knows the disparity between its rhetoric and its actuality, can paradoxically accept imperialism as the price of civilization. Though Marlow admits that "the conquest of the earth" means "taking it away from those who have a different complexion or slightly flatter noses than ourselves," he adds that imperial conquest can be redeemed by "an idea at the back of it; not a sentimental pretense but an idea; and an unselfish belief in the idea — something you can set up, and bow down before, and offer a sacrifice to."

Though ambiguous, *Heart of Darkness* apparently implies that the barbarity of colonialism is preferable to the "darkness" that existed before it. Conrad, through Marlow, qualifies his indictment of imperialism, because he regards colonialism as "a brief and cyclical interruption of the normal predominance of darkness over the course of historical time," writes Ian Watt in his recent, highly-praised study, *Conrad in the Nineteenth Century.*[14] The thin veneer of civilization can crumble at any moment, and man can, as evidenced by Kurtz, sink into the darkness again.

On the other hand, Coppola's colonialists have lost all such illusions. Stripped of any pretense of idealism, not one of the Americans ever attempts to justify the war or talks of progress and civilization. All such talk would be ludicrous, for the Americans swarm over Vietnam killing and burning, not "humanizing, improving, instructing." In Conrad's terms, darkness has come once again, and civilization has descended into barbarism and madness. In fact, darkness and insanity function as recurring, complementary motifs throughout *Apocalypse*

Now. Western civilization has come to a violent end, and nowhere does the movie hint of a way out of the darkness.

Apocalypse Now opens in Saigon, with Willard (Martin Sheen) alone in a dark hotel room waiting for a "mission." Staring up at the ceiling fan, whose rotating blades remind him of helicopters and conjure up apocalyptic fantasies of destruction, he imagines (or remembers) helicopters napalming a jungle as Jim Morrison sings "The End" on the soundtrack. "Saigon ... shit!" he begins his tale, which he calls a "confession." He has just returned to Vietnam from "back there"—meaning a home that no longer exists and a family that he has deserted. "I hardly said a word until I said yes to a divorce," he says, realizing that he can never go home again. So he waits, and on the edge of madness, with nothing to hold him back, Willard slips into a drunken, disorderly frenzy. Smashing his hand into a mirror, he smears blood over his body in a scene that looks forward to and balances the pagan savagery he will later encounter at Kurtz's temple. He desperately needs a mission, for his "sins" as he says, because only some sense of military purpose will keep him from deteriorating into absolute madness.

Willard's mission finally comes—to find and terminate "with extreme expediency" the command of Colonel Walter E. Kurtz. Willard's superiors tell him that Kurtz has gone "insane" but in reviewing Kurtz's impressive career Willard cannot understand why the Army wants him dead. A graduate of Harvard, a veteran of Korea and Vietnam, Kurtz was "being groomed for one of the top spots in the corporation"—before, that is, he began to wage his own war. Willard comes to believe that Kurtz's decision, if he can only understand it, will reveal the secret of this incomprehensible war. Like Marlow's, Willard's journey will be a quest for self-knowledge and meaning. Willard, however, will find neither.

On his journey to the Nang River, which will take him into Cambodia, Willard and his crew come across the smoking ruins of a Vietnamese village laid to waste by Colonel Kilgore, the commander of an air cavalry unit. Kilgore (Robert Duvall) personifies the gung-ho military commander who, as Willard puts it, goes "tear-assing around Nam looking for the shit." Kilgore loves the smell of napalm because it "smells like ... victory," he says. When he sends his helicopters to attack Vietnamese villages, he plays Wagner's *Ride of the Valkyries* over loudspeakers because "it scares hell out of the slopes." Kilgore loves his work, so much so that he remarks sadly to his men: "someday this war's gonna end."

When Willard comes ashore, he asks where he can find the C.O. (a question he will repeat later at the Do Long Bridge, there with a much more ominous response). He finds Kilgore tossing "dead cards" on the corpses "to let Charlie know who killed him." As an amphibious troop carrier razes a village hut and another closes on a group of Vietnamese women and children, a soldier assures the refugees over a bullhorn that "we are your friends." Meanwhile, a television crew films the carnage, and one of the crew shouts to the soldiers "don't look at the camera, just go by like you're fighting." Later, Kilgore throws a party and serves T-bone steaks and beer, and with this Coppola completes his portrait of American policy in Vietnam. That policy, Bogue writes, comes to: "swallow the people, level the land, throw a beach party, and send home footage of Army success."[15]

The air cavalry escort Willard and his crew to the Nang, and they proceed up the dark river. In time they come to Hau Phan, where they find a Playboy Bunny show sponsored by the U.S.O. They watch as scantily and absurdly dressed women dance and contort about a make-shift stage surrounded by huge phallic symbols that take the shape of bullets and bombs. The women taunt the troops mercilessly, mastur-bating with rifles and pistols until the troops can stand it no longer and charge the stage, only to be beaten and tear-gassed by MPs. Under cover of the smoke, the women and their pimping emcee hurriedly depart in a waiting helicopter, leaving the troops angry and frustrated. This scene, equating sex with violence, hints at the perverted, repressed sexuality at the heart of a violent American culture.

The Do Long Bridge, the last outpost before Cambodia, provides Willard and his crew with their most harrowing experience. They ap-proach the bridge at night, with flares and tracers and bullets streaming across the darkness. As the Viet Cong destroy it by night, the Americans rebuild the bridge by day — "just so the generals can say the road's open," one soldier says. Several lost souls try to wade out to the boat; screaming "take me home!" they swirl in the current of the river, as damned as the sinners in Dante's Inferno. Indeed, Willard has come to the final circle of hell but one, and once on shore he finds the American troops holed up in a dark trench strung with Christmas tree lights, with Jimi Hendrix music playing frenetically on a radio. "Who's the commanding officer here?" he asks, as he had done earlier. But this time he receives a different response: "Ain't you?" No one commands at Do Long; all order, all discipline, and all purpose have broken down in a nightmare world of pointless destruction. One machine-gunner, for example, curses hysterically and fires into the darkness, aiming at nothing in particular, just firing into the void. The Do Long Bridge concludes Coppola's por-trait of the war — futile, meaningless, and as horrifying as the pits of hell.

Unfortunately, the last circle of hell — Kurtz and his temple — adds nothing to Coppola's brilliant version of Vietnam. Instead of ending the movie at Do Long, Coppola takes Willard to his murky meeting with Kurtz. Again, Coppola follows Conrad closely; he even includes the incident with the Russian who greets Marlow, here transformed into the photo-journalist (Dennis Hopper) who praises Kurtz and tells how the "poet warrior" has "enlarged" his mind. But Coppola so overdoes the decapitated heads and the paganism that the meeting with Kurtz proves anticlimactic. As Kurtz, Marlon Brando mumbles gibberish, quotes T.S. Eliot, and generally sounds more like Brando playing guru than Conrad's Kurtz. Brando/Kurtz rambles on about the need for "horror" and "moral terror" in the conduct of the war, recalling a tape he had made earlier: "we must kill them, we must incinerate them, pig after pig, cow after cow, village after village, army after army." After all this Willard finally puts him out of his misery, but not before he utters "the horror — the horror." And as we expect from our knowledge of Conrad, Willard finds where Kurtz had scribbled "Drop the bomb. Exterminate them all."

Most critics agree with Peter Marin, who finds the last third of *Apocalypse Now* "a pastiche of borrowed meanings and second-hand myths, in which Coppola, striving to locate the significance of his work, loses his way completely."[16] On the other hand, Bogue finds the conclusion consistent with Coppola's theme. He argues that Coppola exaggerates Kurtz and his mystical gibberish in order "to deflate him, to expose him as a poseur and a sham."[17] Bogue contrasts Willard's failure to find any substance in the ravings of Kurtz with Marlow's revelation at the end of *Heart of Darkness*: "Because Kurtz faces his inner darkness, Marlow finds him a remarkable man. His judgment on himself is 'some sort of belief' which has 'the appalling face of a glimpsed truth'; his is 'an affirmation, a moral victory, paid for by innumerable defeats, by abominable terrors, by abominable satisfactions.'"[18] In contrast, Willard learns nothing from Kurtz; he finds no wisdom and no moral, no method to Kurtz's madness. Thus Bogue insists that *Apocalypse Now* was intended, and should be seen, as a "failed quest."

Though I agree in part with Bogue, his argument does not refute the criticism of *Apocalypse Now*. Whether or not Coppola intended his movie to be a "failed quest" does not alter the fact that the majority of critics and viewers find the conclusion unsatisfactory — thematically confused, overly-literary, and inconsistent with the rest of the movie. Also, Coppola made a serious mistake by revising the final scene of the movie to suit his financial backers. The original conclusion, the one seen at the official screening at Cannes, shows Willard coming out of the temple and being approached by Kurtz's followers: the pagans will need a new leader, and they look to Willard hopefully... Willard pauses, considering. The intended meaning is clear; Willard can never go back to civilization, for he has tried to go home before, and he knows that (as he says) "it just doesn't exist anymore."

Willard understands, as does Kurtz, the madness of Vietnam, a war of "insanity and murder" that makes a lie out of morality and civilization itself. "Charging someone with murder in this place is like handing out tickets at the Indianapolis 500," Willard says. Kurtz, too, had made the same statement when he asked "what do they call it when the assassins accuse the assassin?" Ironically, the pursuit of victory in Vietnam has led to the extinction of civilization, to the apocalypse. That grim truth represents the "heart of darkness" in *Apocalypse Now.*

Only *Hearts and Minds*, Peter Davis' highly-acclaimed documentary of the Vietnam War, equals *Apocalypse Now* in importance. Primarily because of Davis' craftsmanship, and his stature in the film community, *Hearts and Minds* has enjoyed a much wider audience than other Vietnam documentaries (most of them low-budget, privately-produced anti-war films). Even so, *Hearts and Minds* has had a controversial history, as have Davis' other films—*Hunger in America*, and the Emmy-winning *The Selling of the Pentagon.* On this film Davis worked with Bert Schneider, who was under a multi-picture contract with Columbia and who had produced such commercially successful movies as *Easy Rider, The Last Picture Show,* and *Five Easy Pieces.* Schneider produced *Hearts and Minds* for Columbia, and the film appeared to be another success when it won rave reviews at the 1974 Cannes Festival. However, Columbia, fearing political backlash, refused to acknowledge its support or to distribute the movie. In response, Davis and Schneider began showing the film to sympathetic reviewers, and public pressure mounted for its release. The deadlock was broken only when a private purchasing company (Rainbow) bought the film from Columbia and signed a contract with Warners for its distribution.

Just then, Walt Rostow, an important interviewee in *Hearts and Minds,* apparently realized what a fool he had made of himself on film and secured a court order preventing it from being shown. Warners, Rainbow, Davis, and Schneider all fought the injunction, and they managed to get it reversed in January 1975. When the movie finally reached the screen, popular and critical response was highly favorable. However, the controversy continued later that year at the Academy Awards ceremonies, where *Hearts and Minds* received an Academy Award for the year's best documentary. Breaking with the usual banality of the award ceremony, Schneider unexpectedly celebrated the victory of the Vietnamese revolution and even read a telegram from a representative of the Progressive Revolutionary Government (Viet Cong) of Vietnam. Schneider's "outburst" precipitated a second "outburst" from academy officials, none of whom wished to be associated with Schneider's political statement. Bob Hope quickly drafted a disclaimer, and Frank Sinatra just as quickly read the disclaimer to the live television audience over the strong objections of Shirley MacLaine and others.

The controversy surrounding *Hearts and Minds* testifies to the emotional power of the film. The movie differs from the traditional documentary in that director Davis does not conceal his political bias; in fact, he intends the film to evoke feelings of pity and anger — pity at the plight of the Vietnamese people, and anger at the arrogant American culture that ravaged them. To achieve the necessary depth, Davis combines actual newsreel footage of the war with long interviews of government and military officials as well as civilians, both American and Vietnamese. Davis includes footage of presidents from Truman through Nixon pledging to carry on the war, and he contrasts the statements of prowar spokesmen like General William Westmoreland and Rostow with the statements of antiwar spokesmen like William Fulbright and Robert Kennedy. In fact, *Hearts and Minds* works by a method of ironic juxtaposition, with Davis cutting rapidly from scene to scene and from interview to interview in a way that allows him to comment on his subject.

For example, Davis contradicts the statements of the five U.S. presidents by including an interview with Daniel Ellsberg, who recounts a detailed history of American involvement in Vietnam; and he contradicts the promises of military victory made by various public officials by including an interview with former Secretary of Defense Clark Clifford, who recounts his experience negotiating with generals who, while promising victory, requested more and more troops. Davis films General Westmoreland proclaiming that the Vietnamese do not value human life, and he follows Westmoreland's comment by filming a Vietnamese father weeping hysterically over the death of his child — killed by American bombs.

In other scenes and interviews the irony is inherent, as when an American general talks about the courage of his "churchgoing" troops and concludes by saying that "they're a bloody good bunch of killers." Davis repeatedly undermines the prowar position by exposing the disparity between the rhetoric of American officials and the actual devastation of the war, calling into question the very integrity of those officials.

Hearts and Minds also explores the roots of American involvement in Vietnam in terms of a psychological predisposition to violence in American culture. Davis interviews athletes and military personnel, and he films football games, marching bands, military parades, and Fourth of July celebrations — all of which he sees as expressing an insensitive, militaristic culture. One of the most moving moments in the film occurs during the interview of a former pilot who tells of his experience flying bombing missions over North and South Vietnam. The pilot talks about the military technology that enabled him and the other Americans to kill from longrange so precisely, so perfectly. Back then, the pilot says, the war seemed to be only an exercise in high technology, but now he has begun to wonder what it must have been like for the people below his bombs. What would he think, he asks himself, if his children were napalmed? He begins to weep, thinking of his own children, and all the other children. The moment is a triumph, for the pilot has managed to see through the rhetoric and the abstractions of official propaganda to the human reality of the war—what the war meant in terms of human suffering. That simple but elusive realization is what Peter Davis intends to foster in *Hearts and Minds*.

Hearts and Minds and *Apocalypse Now* are the most important of Hollywood's excursions into the difficult subject of Vietnam; both reveal the more horrifying aspects of the war and make powerful public statements about the brutality of the culture that waged it. The other films— *Coming Home* and *The Deer Hunter* included—have packaged and sold Vietnam as a sentimental soap opera in order to insure commercial success. Even more than the literature, the Vietnam movies generally have derealized Vietnam to the point of unrecognizability.

Chapter 11. Conclusion

> ... this is the finis, the end of man in
> this clearing, this opening in the jungle,
> the end of humankind itself and the
> planet earth on which it abides. —
> William Eastlake, The Bamboo Bed.

It is only fitting that this discussion should return, ultimately, to *The Quiet American*. Not only did Graham Greene's short novel predict the failure of American intervention in Vietnam, it revealed certain brutal truths about American culture that appear even more true today. For Greene, through Alden Pyle and his other fictional quiet Americans, portrays the arrogance and the brutality of a messianic culture that claims the right to eradicate older cultures in the name of such fictions as "national democracy." With their political jingoism and their moral banalities, Greene's quiet Americans feel so assured of their superiority that they can justify everything from rigged elections to mass murder by paying lip service to slogans like "democracy" and "progress." These Americans prove insensitive to human life, and to the suffering and death caused by their nation-building schemes. Writing for *Harper's* in 1980 about the American experience in Vietnam, Peter Marin comes to the same conclusion that Greene did 24 years earlier: all of us, Marin argues, have "trouble grasping the pain and death incumbent upon us, or the cost to others of our careless posturing, arrogance, and rage."[1]

Significantly, most recent Vietnam War literature and films share this dark vision of America. Often the Vietnam experience becomes a metaphor for America: a brutal culture that exports its violence to distant lands in Southeast Asia. What's more, the best of the Vietnam books and films actually examine the cultural causes of American brutality. Here I would include personal narratives like Michael Herr's *Dispatches*, Ron Kovic's *Born on the Fourth of July*, and Philip Caputo's *A Rumor of War*; novels like Robert Stone's *Dog Soldiers*, Tim O'Brien's *Going After Cacciato*, Charles Durden's *No Bugles, No Drums*, David Halberstam's *One Very Hot Day*, Victor Kolpacoff's *The Prisoners of Quai Dong*, and William Eastlake's *The Bamboo Bed*[2]; and movies like Francis Ford Coppola's *Apocalypse Now* and Peter Davis' *Hearts and Minds*. These writers and directors arrive at remarkably similar conclusions, both as to the causes of American brutality, and why it erupted in Vietnam.

First, some writers and directors depict the war as resulting from misguided political assumptions that led the United States deeper and deeper into a war that could not be won. Mired in a futile war, Americans reacted with anger and excessive force against the Vietnamese people and sank irrevocably into the abyss of an immoral war. For example, in *A Rumor of War* Philip Caputo blames the "illusions" and the "intoxicating atmosphere" of the Kennedy years for the "tragifarce" of Vietnam. Kennedy, it seems, inspired a "missionary idealism," and Caputo and his generation found themselves "ordained to play cop to the Communists' robber and spread our political faith around the world."[3] That misguided idealism quickly "corroded" in Vietnam, as the war became a war of attrition and degenerated into savagery.

"Out there," Caputo writes, "lacking restraints, sanctioned to kill, confronted by a hostile country and a relentless enemy, we sank into a brutish state."[4] Tim O'Brien's *Going After Cacciato*, David Halberstam's *One Very Hot Day*, and Victor Kolpacoff's *The Prisoners of Quai Dong* all share Caputo's view that corrupted idealism and frustration led to the savagery and inhumanity of the war. So, too, does Michael Cimino's movie, *The Deer Hunter*, though in a much more self-pitying way.

Other writers and directors regard Vietnam as an act of insanity, the ultimate extension of an insane culture. Norman Mailer comes to this conclusion in *Why Are We in Vietnam?* (1967) and *The Armies of the Night* (1968). In his novel, *Why Are We in Vietnam?*, Mailer creates a collection of deranged characters that together provide a psychological barometer of America's psychic problems. Ronald, for example, is "morally anesthetized, and smoldering with presumptive violence ... a humdinger of a latent homosexual highly over-heterosexual with onanistic narcissistic and sodomistic overtones."⁵ Likewise, D.J. and Tex, two red-blooded American youths as eager to go hunting Cong in Vietnam as bear in Alaska, suffer from a host of psychosexual deformities, sadistic instincts and outright psychoses. Both of them prove "a most peculiar blendaroon of humanity and evil, technological know-how, pure savagery, sweet aching secret American youth, and sheer downright meanness." Wallowing in the "essential animal insanity of things," they go off at the end of the novel "to see the wizard in Vietnam."⁶

Mailer clarifies this admittedly overstated portrait of insanity in his highly acclaimed narrative, *The Armies of the Night* — a book that won both the Pulitzer Prize and the National Book Award. "He had come to the saddest conclusion of all," he writes there, characteristically speaking of himself in the third person, "for it went beyond the war in Vietnam. He had come to decide that the center of America might be insane. The country had been living with a controlled, even fiercely controlled, schizophrenia which had been deepening with the years." Mailer goes on to argue that this schizophrenia resulted from the contradiction betweeen "Christianity" and the "corporation" and "had brought the country to a state of suppressed schizophrenia so deep that the foul brutalities of the war in Vietnam were the only temporary cure possible for the condition — since the expression of brutality offers a definite if temporary relief to the schizophrenic. So the average good Christian American secretly loved the war in Vietnam. It opened his emotions. He felt compassion," while he witnessed and supported the killing. An arm-chair murderer.

In *Dispatches*, Michael Herr chronicles a similar madness. From his descriptions of the deadly technology that could destroy Vietnam but could not win the war, to his portraits of the "bunch of dumb, brutal killers" who did the actual killing, Herr provides a horrifying account of an insensitive American culture. Herr links the insanity of the war to the insanity of the culture itself, all the deluded Americans who had "seen too many movies, stayed too long in Television City." The American soldiers knew "the madness, the bitterness, the horror and doom" of Vietnam. "They were hip to it, and more: they savored it. It was no more insane than most of what was going down." So "people retreated into positions of hard irony, cynicism, despair, some saw the action and

declared for it, only heavy killing could make them feel so alive."[8] Both
Herr and Mailer agree, so does William Eastlake in *The Bamboo Bed*: the
killing in Vietnam provided an outlet for the insane. Francis Ford Coppola's movie, *Apocalypse Now*, documents this same insanity.

Still other writers and directors interpret Vietnam as a symptom of a
predatory or imperialistic culture. The war, they argue, was fought
primarily to exploit an underdeveloped nation, an act of imperialist
aggression that no amount of propaganda could conceal. These writers
stress the link between advanced consumer capitalism and the war in
Vietnam. For example, Charles Durden presents the war in *No Bugles,
No Drums* as a kind of lethal merchandise sold to a consumer society so
that the "thieves" and "war profiteers" can earn their profits — for these
people turn a handsome profit on "free-fire zones" and "legal murder," just
as they do on "Fords" and "mass production." Robert Stone makes this
same connection in *Dog Soldiers*, where the character of Antheil personifies the predatory nature of advanced consumer capitalism. While
countless Americans die in the jungles of Vietnam, Antheil garners
enormous profits for the booming heroin trade occasioned by the war.
To Antheil, the victims he sacrifices in Vietnam are expendable "meat,"
packaged in coffins and shipped back to the United States. Ron Kovic
comes to a similar conclusion in *Born on the Fourth of July*, as does
George Davis in the novel *Coming Home* and Peter Davis in his
documentary film, *Hearts and Minds*.

Despite their differing accounts of the origins of the war, almost all
Vietnam writers and directors share an apocalyptic vision of its end.
With William Eastlake in *The Bamboo Bed*, they present Vietnam as "the
finis, the end of man in this clearing, this opening in the jungle, the end of
humankind itself and the planet earth on which it abides." The mass
destruction in Vietnam prompts Eastlake to ask, sarcastically: "you don't
think man will prevail? You should see him behave in Asia.... That is
what people do not realize about this war. They do not realize it is a war
to end war. The end of man."[9] Much later, of course, Francis Ford Coppola popularized this vision in *Apocalypse Now*, his attempt to make an
epic movie of the Vietnam War. Appropriately, the movie opens with a
panoramic shot of a dense green jungle that suddenly explodes into
flames, as Jim Morrison chants "this is the end, my friends, of all that's
ever been, the end...." Not even the gratuitous ending can completely
detract from the brilliant opening sequences of the movie, which succeed
in synthesizing a longstanding interpretation of Vietnam.

The apocalyptic vision of the Vietnam books and films differs
radically (and perhaps ironically) from the traditional biblical meaning
of apocalypse. No trace of revelation exists in these works, no possibility
of prophetic disclosure after the destruction of the old order, no faith in a

future when all things will be revealed in their true nature. Instead, the world born in Vietnam becomes a monstrosity of senseless violence and random destruction, a "physical universe" that Robert Stone describes in *Dog Soldiers* as "capable of composing itself, at any time and without notice, into a massive instrument of agonizing death."[10] Out of this collective vision comes a literature and a cinema of despair laced with death. "Everything I see is blown through with smoke, everything is on fire everywhere," Michael Herr writes in *Dispatches*. "It doesn't matter that memory distorts; every image, every sound comes back out of smoke and the smell of things burning."[11] The end, then, is physical annihilation, purely and simply.

Perhaps even more ominously, the Vietnam writers and directors imply the destruction of human values and human morality. The "organized butchery" of the war that Philip Caputo describes in *A Rumor of War* makes a mockery of all values and reduces man to the level of an animal "soaring high, very high in a delirium of violence."[12] A sense of camaraderie and a desperate courage become the only possible values in a world where man lives day to day on the brink of extinction, killing and waiting to be killed. In this world nothing matters except survival — not the value and integrity of human life, not principles and long-forgotten causes, not ethics and morality. Lost in the free-fire zone of Vietnam, "living dogs lived. It was all they knew."[13] This line from *Dog Soldiers* provides a fitting epitaph for the collective vision, the shared memory of Vietnam.

Not that these writers and directors hold the war entirely responsible for the destruction of values. Rather, the war contributed to and illustrated the destruction, revealed it in its most undeniable form in the jungles of Vietnam. As a symptom of the destruction, the war reflects cultural crisis. It may well be, as cultural historians like Christopher Lasch and Gerald Graff have argued, that advanced consumer capitalism itself has eroded all values and made debacles like Vietnam possible, perhaps inevitable. Either writer would likely agree that "the essence of capitalistic reality is its unreality, its malleable, ephemeral quality"[14] — the same elusive unreality that one finds in the official accounts of the war in Vietnam. Gerald Graff, in particular, argues that advanced consumer capitalism has a "built-in need to destroy all vestiges of tradition, all orthodox ideologies, all continuous forms of reality in order to stimulate higher levels of consumption."[15] For example, the family, the church, and other stabilizing institutions have to be undermined in order to promote fads such as consumer sex and consumer alienation.

The same holds true of Vietnam, where history and culture had to be negated in order to mass market the consumer entity known as South

Vietnam. By promoting continuous discontinuity through its exploitation of fashion and ephemeral novelty, our consumer society and
its "cult of consumption" effects a systematic derangement of the senses.
The attack on all forms of continuity results in "the waning belief in the
reality of the external world" and "the waning of the sense of historical
time," Lasch argues in *The Culture of Narcissism*.[15] Thus the culture of
narcissism is born: a culture composed of isolated individuals, victims of
a culturally conditioned alienation, estranged from external reality, from
history, and from binding values.

The Vietnam writers and film directors reflect these losses. In fact,
their portraits of Vietnam take to an extreme the unreality, the discontinuity, and the loss of values that may characterize much of our experience in America today. These creative efforts affirm very little, can
not replace all that has been destroyed in Vietnam—they simply record
the losses. Taken as a whole, these works are as nihilistic as any ever
produced in America. Michael Herr concludes *Dispatches* with his return
to America and "going down again into the sucking mud of the culture."[17]
In *A Rumor of War*, Philip Caputo retreats into the cynicism of the
inevitability of "the next generation ... being crucified in the next war."[18]
And Ron Kovic adds two lines to the end of *Born on the Fourth of July*:
"It was all sort of easy. / It had all come and gone."[19]

Vietnam remains an open sore on the American national consciousness, a wound that has not healed because Americans have refused to
acknowledge it, let alone heal it. Gustav Hasford, Vietnam veteran and
writer, addressed our evasion of the war in a recent article in *The Los
Angeles Times*. "What have I learned about Vietnam from the federal
government?" Hasford asked. "I have learned, for one thing, that politics
is a ballet of devils and that politicians, with paper roses falling out of
their mouths, cannot conceal the blood from distant wounds that stains
their neckties—but they do try, and millions do listen and believe and
choose not to see.[20] By listening to the Vietnam veterans and not to the
politicians who tell us about the "noble cause" of Vietnam, we can finally
take the first step toward confronting what we did in Southeast Asia. The
Vietnam books and films can also help us in our effort to understand the
war, for these works provide a cultural record of our attempts—our successes, as well as our failures—to come to terms with Vietnam. If we try,
we can save the next generation from being crucified a decade from now
in distant lands whose names we barely recognize now. We can prevent
another misbegotten war.

Chapter Notes

Chapter 1

[1]Michael Herr, *Dispatches* (New York: Knopf, 1977), p. 244.

[2]All statistics in this chapter are taken from *Setting the Stage*, Volume I of *The Vietnam Experience*, eds. Edward Doyle and Samuel Lipsman (Boston: Boston Publishing Co., 1981).

[3]As quoted by Phillip Knightley in *The First Casualty* (New York: Harcourt Brace Jovanovich, 1975), p. 373.

[4]Peter Marin, "Coming to Terms with Vietnam," *Harper's*, December 1980, p. 41.

[5]Walter LaFeber, "The Last War, the Next War, and the New Revisionists," *Democracy* 1 (January 1981), p. 93.

[6]Noam Chomsky, *After the Cataclysm* (Boston: South End Press, 1979), p. x.

[7]Chomsky, p. 6.

[8]LaFeber, p. 98.

[9]Gloria Emerson, *Winners and Losers* (New York: Random House, 1976), p. 112.

[10]Emerson, p. 4.

[11]Frances Fitzgerald, *Fire in the Lake* (Boston: Little, Brown, 1972), p. 422.

[12]Charles Durden, *No Bugles, No Drums* (New York: Viking, 1976), p. 166.

[13]Marin, p. 42.

[14]Saul Maloff, "Vietnam Mon Amour," *Commonweal*, February 3, 1978, p. 84.

[15]Marin, pp. 42-43.

Chapter 2

[1]Gloria Emerson, *Winners and Losers* (New York: Random House, 1976), p. 298.

[2]Gloria Emerson, "Our Man in Antibes: Graham Greene," *Rolling Stone*, March 9, 1978, p. 45.

[3]Zalin Grant, "Vietnam as Fable," *The New Republic*, March 25, 1978, p. 24.

[4]Gordon O. Taylor, "American Personal Narrative of the War in Vietnam," *American Literature*, 54, (May 1980), p. 294.

[5]Graham Greene, *The Quiet American* (New York: Viking, 1956), p. 40. All further references to *The Quiet American* will be to this edition; page numbers will be cited parenthetically in the text.

[6]Taylor, p. 303.

[7]Michael Herr, *Dispatches* (New York: Knopf, 1977), p. 188.

[8]As quoted in Emerson, *Winners and Losers*, p. 299.

Chapter 3

[1]Gloria Emerson, *Winners and Losers* (New York: Random House, 1976), p. 280.

[2]Emerson, p. 299.

[3]Bernard Fall, *Last Reflections on a War* (New York: Doubleday, 1967), p. 137.

[4]As quoted by Guenter Lewy in *America in Vietnam* (New York: Oxford University Press, 1978), p. 12.

[5]As quoted by Archimedes L.A. Patti in *Why Viet Nam?* (Berkeley: University of California Press, 1980), p. 424.

[6]Patti, p. 388.

[7]Patti, p. 388.

[8]Patti, p. 448.

[9]Gareth Porter, *Vietnam: A History in Documents* (New York: New American Library, 1981), p. xxviii.

[10]Porter, p. xxviii.

[11]Porter, p. 63.

[12]Frances Fitzgerald, *Fire in the Lake* (Boston: Little, Brown, 1972), pp. 66-7.

[13]Fitzgerald, p. 67.

[14]Fall, p. 143.

[15]Fitzgerald, p. 76.

[16]Porter, p. 161.

[17]Porter, p. 179.

[18]Fitzgerald, p. 69.

[19]Fall, p. 145.

[20]Fitzgerald, p. 78.

[21]Fitzgerald, p. 317.

[22]As quoted by Phillip Knightley in *The First Casualty* (New York: Harcourt Brace Jovanovich, 1975), p. 374.

[23]Fitzgerald, p. 73.

[24]Fitzgerald, p. 87.

[25]Fitzgerald, p. 72.

[26]Fitzgerald, pp. 89, 90.

[27]Fitzgerald, p. 92.

[28]Porter, pp. 240-1.

[29]Porter, p. 242.

[30]Porter, p. 254.

[31]As quoted by Edward Doyle and Samuel Lipsman, eds., in *Setting the Stage,* Volume I of *The Vietnam Experience* (Boston: Boston Publishing Co., 1981), p. 21.

[32]Doyle and Lipsman, p. 21.

[33]As quoted by Noam Chomsky in *After the Cataclysm* (Boston: South End Press, 1979), p. 8.

[34]Fitzgerald, pp. 364-5.

[35]C.D.B. Bryan, *Friendly Fire* (New York: Putnam's, 1976), p. 190.

[36]Knightley, p. 376.

[37]Bryan, p. 277.

[38]Fitzgerald, p. 363.

[39]Michael Herr, *Dispatches* (New York: Knopf, 1977), p. 214.

[40]Gerald Graff, *Literature Against Itself* (Chicago: University of Chicago Press, 1979), p. 204.

[41]Robert Stone, *Dog Soldiers* (Boston: Houghton Mifflin, 1974), p. 125.

[42]Charles Durden, *No Bugles, No Drums* (New York: Viking Press, 1976), p. 127.

Chapter 4

[1]Michael Herr, *Dispatches* (New York: Knopf, 1977), p. 214.

[2]Herr, pp. 49-50.

[3]Tim O'Brien, *If I Die in a Combat Zone* (New York: Delacorte, 1973), pp. 139-40.

[4]Phillip Knightley, *The First Casualty* (New York: Harcourt Brace Jovanovich, 1975), p. 375.

[5]Knightley, p. 378.

[6]Knightley, p. 379.

[7]Herr, p. 214.

[8]Herr, p. 214.

[9]Knightley, p. 379.

[10]As quoted in Knightley, p. 389.

[11]Herr, p. 229.

[12]Herr, pp. 143, 145.

[13]Herr, p. 71.

[14]Knightley, p. 390.

[15]As quoted by Knightley, p. 423.

[16]Knightley, p. 415.

[17]Jonathan Schell, "The Village of Ben Suc," *The New Yorker*, July 15, 1967, p. 50.

[18]Schell, p. 56.

[19]Schell, p. 58.

[20]Schell, p. 92.

Chapter 5

[1]Robin Moore, *The Green Berets* (New York: Crown, 1965), p. 1. All further references to *The Green Berets* will be to this edition; page numbers will be cited parenthetically.

[2]Peter Marin, "Coming to Terms with Vietnam," *Harper's*, December 1980, p. 48.

[3]Michael Herr, *Dispatches* (New York: Knopf, 1977), p. 188.

[4]Though one could also make the same criticism of Robert Roth's *Sand in the Wind* (1973) or James Webb's *Fields of Fire* (1978), for example.

[5]P.S. Prescott, review of *Better Times Than These*, *Newsweek*, June 19, 1978, p. 80.

[6]William Turner Huggett, *Body Count* (New York: Putnam's, 1973), p. 30. All further references to *Body Count* will be to this edition; page numbers will be cited parenthetically.

[7]Winston Groom, *Better Times Than These* (New York: Summit Books, 1978), p. 409.

[8]Asa Baber, *The Land of a Million Elephants* (New York: Morrow, 1970).

Chapter 6

[1]Zalin Grant, "Vietnam as Fable," *The New Republic*, March 25, 1978, p. 24.

[2]Mark Baker, *Nam* (New York: Morrow, 1981), p. 49.

[3]Charles Durden, *No Bugles, No Drums* (New York: Viking Press, 1976), p. 207. All further references to *No Bugles, No Drums* will be to this edition; page numbers will be cited parenthetically.

[4]Pearl K. Bell, "Writing About Vietnam," *Commentary*, October 1978, p. 77.

[5]C.D.B. Bryan, "The Different War," *New York Times Book Review*, November 20, 1977, p. 1.

[6]Michael Herr, *Dispatches* (New York: Knopf, 1977), p. 20. All further references to *Dispatches* will be to this edition; page numbers will be cited parenthetically.

[7]John Hellman, "The New Journalism and Vietnam: Memory as Structure in Michael Herr's *Dispatches*," *South Atlantic Quarterly* 79 (Spring 1980), p. 142.

[8]Philip Caputo, *A Rumor of War* (New York: Holt, Rinehart & Winston, 1977), p. xix.

[9]Josiah Bunting, *The Lionheads* (New York: Braziller, 1972), p. 112.

[10]William Eastlake, *The Bamboo Bed* (New York: Simon & Schuster, 1969), p. 334.

[11]Philip D. Beidler, "Truth-Telling and Literary Values in the Vietnam Novel," *South Atlantic Quarterly* 78 (Spring 1979), p. 151.

[12]Beidler, p. 151.

[13]Gustav Hasford, *The Short-Timers* (New York: Harper & Row, 1979), p. 38, 78.

[14]Gerald Graff, *Literature Against Itself* (Chicago: University of Chicago Press, 1979), p. 238.

Chapter 7

[1]As quoted by Phillip Knightley in *The First Casualty* (New York: Harcourt Brace Jovanovich, 1975), p. 423.

[2]William Eastlake, *The Bamboo Bed* (New York: Simon & Schuster, 1969), p. 128.

[3]David Halberstam, *One Very Hot Day* (Boston: Houghton Mifflin, 1967), p. 68. All further references to *One Very Hot Day* will be to this edition; page numbers will be cited parenthetically.

[4]Gloria Emerson, *Winners and Losers* (New York: Random House, 1976), p. 195.

[5]Tim O'Brien, *Going After Cacciato* (New York: Delacorte, 1978), p. 41. All further references to *Going After Cacciato* will be to this edition; page numbers will be cited parenthetically.

[6]Arthur M. Saltzman, "The Betrayal of the Imagination: Paul Brodeur's *The Stunt Man* and Tim O'Brien's *Going After Cacciato*," *Critique* 22, 1 (1980), pp. 36-37.

[7]Tim O'Brien, *If I Die in a Combat Zone* (New York: Delacorte, 1973), p. 167.

[8]O'Brien, *If I Die*, p. 168.

Chapter 8

[1]Michael Herr, *Dispatches* (New York: Knopf, 1977), p. 226.

[2]Tim O'Brien, *If I Die in a Combat Zone* (New York: Delacorte, 1973), pp. 133 and 22.

[3]Tim O'Brien, *Going After Cacciato* (New York: Delacorte, 1978), p. 322.

[4]Philip Caputo, *A Rumor of War* (New York: Holt, Rinehart & Winston, 1977), p. 230. All further references to *A Rumor of War* will be to this edition; page numbers will be cited parenthetically.

[5]Zalin Grant, "Vietnam as Fable," *The New Republic*, March 25, 1978, p. 23.

[6]Victor Kolpacoff, *The Prisoners of Quai Dong* (New York: New American Library, 1967), p. 45. All further references to *The Prisoners of Quai Dong* will be to this edition; page numbers will be cited parenthetically.

[7]Joseph A. Tetlow, "The Vietnam War Novel," *America*, July 1980, p. 34.

[8]Robert Stone, *Dog Soldiers* (Boston: Houghton Mifflin, 1974), p. 7. All further references to *Dog Soldiers* will be to this edition; page numbers will be cited parenthetically.

Pearl K. Bell, "Writing About Vietnam," *Commentary*, October 1978, p. 77.

[10]Peter Marin, "Coming to Terms with Vietnam," *Harper's*, December 1980, p. 50.

Chapter 9

[1]Michael Herr, *Dispatches* (New York: Knopf, 1977), p. 207.

[2]Philip Caputo, *A Rumor of War* (New York: Holt, Rinehart & Winston, 1977), pp. 223-24.

[3]Mark Baker, *Nam* (New York: Morrow, 1981), p. 291.

[4]Ronald J. Glasser, *365 Days* (New York: Braziller, 1971), p. 5.

[5]C.D.B. Bryan, *Friendly Fire* (New York: Putnam's, 1976), p. 330.

[6]Baker, p. 262.

[7]William Eastlake, *The Bamboo Bed* (New York: Simon & Schuster, 1969), p. 139.

[8]Ron Kovic, *Born on the Fourth of July* (New York: McGraw-Hill, 1976), p. 114. All further references to *Born on the Fourth of July* will be to this edition; page numbers will be cited parenthetically.

[9]Charles Durden, *No Bugles, No Drums* (New York: Viking Press, 1976), p. 210. All further references to *No Bugles, No Drums* will be to this edition; page numbers will be cited parenthetically.

[10]Robert Stone, *Dog Soldiers* (Boston: Houghton Mifflin, 1974), p. 110. All further references to *Dog Soldiers* will be to this edition; page numbers will be cited parenthetically.

[11]George Davis, *Coming Home* (New York: Random House, 1971), p. 88. All further references to *Coming Home* will be to this edition; page numbers will be cited parenthetically.

Chapter 10

[1]Al Auster and Leonard Quart, "Hollywood and Vietnam: The Will," *Cineaste* 9 (Spring 1979), p. 5.

[2]John Pym, "A Bullet in the Head: Vietnam Remembered," *Sight and Sound* 48 (Spring 1979), p. 83.

[3]William J. Palmer, "The Vietnam War Films," *Film Library Quarterly* 13 (4 1980), p. 7.

[4]Palmer, p. 7.

[5]Auster and Quart, p. 4.

[6]Peter Marin, "Coming to Terms with Vietnam," *Harper's*, December 1980, p. 45.

[7]As quoted in Auster and Quart, p. 9.

[8]Palmer, p. 9.

[9]Auster and Quart, p. 9.

[10]Marin, p. 46.

[11]Marin, pp. 46-47.

[12]Ronald L. Bogue, "The Heartless Darkness of *Apocalypse Now*," *The Georgia Review* 35 (Fall 1981), p. 612.

[13]Bogue, p. 613.

[14]Ian Watt, *Conrad in the Nineteenth Century* (Berkeley: University of California Press, 1979), p. 216.

[15]Bogue, p. 616.

[16]Marin, p. 47.

[17]Bogue, p. 623.

[18]Bogue, pp. 618-19.

Chapter 11

[1]Peter Marin, "Coming to Terms with Vietnam," *Harper's*, December 1980, p. 56.

[2]So, too, do Gloria Emerson in *Winners and Losers* and Frances Fitzgerald in *Fire in the Lake*, though these writers approach the problem differently — Emerson through the stories of people whose lives were irrevocably affected by the war, and Fitzgerald through the actual history of the conflagration.

[3]Philip Caputo, *A Rumor of War* (New York: Holt, Rinehart & Winston, 1977), p. xii.

[4]Caputo, p. xviii.

[5]Norman Mailer, *Why Are We in Vietnam?* (New York: Putnam's, 1967), p. 14.

[6]Mailer, *Why Are We in Vietnam?*, p. 162, 70 and 208.

[7]Norman Mailer, *The Armies of the Night* (New York: New American Library, 1968), p. 188.

[8]Michael Herr, *Dispatches* (New York: Knopf, 1977), pp. 207, 209, 102 and 58.

[9]William Eastlake, *The Bamboo Bed* (New York: Simon & Schuster, 1969), pp. 33-34, and 250.

[10]Robert Stone, *Dog Soldiers* (Boston: Houghton Mifflin, 1974), p. 185.

[11]Herr, p. 146.

[12]Caputo, p. 269.

[13]Stone, p. 186.

[14]Gerald Graff, *Literature Against Itself* (Chicago: University of Chicago Press, 1979), p. 8.

[15]Graff, p. 8.

[16]Christopher Lasch, *The Culture of Narcissism* (New York: Norton, 1978), pp. 90 and 5.

[17]Herr, p. 258.

[18]Caputo, p. xix.

[19]Ron Kovic, *Born on the Fourth of July* (New York: McGraw-Hill, 1976), p. 208.

[20]As quoted by Gareth Porter, ed., in *Vietnam, A History in Documents* (New York: New American Library, 1981), p. xxvi.

Bibliography

Novels

Baber, Asa. *The Land of a Million Elephants.* New York: William Morrow Co., 1970.

Ballard, J.G. *Crash.* New York: Farrar, Straus & Giroux, 1973.

Briley, John. *The Traitors.* New York: G.P. Putnam's Sons, 1969.

Brodeur, Paul. *The Stunt Man.* New York: Atheneum, 1970.

Bunting, Josiah. *The Lionheads.* New York: George Braziller, 1972.

Burdick, Eugene, and William J. Lederer. *The Ugly American.* New York: W.W. Norton, 1958.

Butler, Robert Olen. *The Alleys of Eden.* New York: Horizon Press, 1981.

Cassidy, John. *A Station in the Delta.* New York: Charles Scribner's Sons, 1979.

Connolly, Edward. *Deer Run.* New York: Charles Scribner's Sons, 1971.

Crumley, James. *One to Count Cadence.* New York: Random House, 1969.

Davis, George. *Coming Home.* New York: Random House, 1971.

Dunn, Mary Lois. *The Man in the Box.* New York: McGraw-Hill, 1968.

Durden, Charles. *No Bugles, No Drums.* New York: Viking Press, 1976.

Eastlake, William. *The Bamboo Bed.* New York: Simon & Schuster, 1969.

Ellison, James Whitfield. *The Summer After the War.* New York: Dodd, Mead, 1972.

Ford, Daniel. *Incident at Muc Wa.* New York: Doubleday, 1967.

Giovannitti, Len. *The Man Who Won the Medal of Honor.* New York: Random House, 1973.

Gottlieb, Linda, and Joan Silver. *Limbo.* New York: Viking Press, 1972.

Graham, Gail. *Cross-Fire.* New York: Pantheon, 1972.

Groom, Winston. *Better Times Than These.* New York: Summit Books, 1978.

Halberstam, David. *One Very Hot Day.* Boston: Houghton Mifflin, 1967.

Haldeman, Joe W. *War Year.* New York: Holt, Rinehart & Winston, 1972.

Hasford, Gustav. *The Short-Timers.* New York: Harper & Row, 1979.

Heinemann, Larry. *Close Quarters.* New York: Farrar, Straus & Giroux, 1974.

Huggett, William Turner. *Body Count.* New York: G.P. Putnam's Sons, 1973.

Kolpacoff, Victor. *The Prisoners of Quai Dong.* New York: New American Library, 1967.

Kozak, Yitka R. *The Conscientious Objector.* Jericho, N.Y.: Exposition, 1973.

Little, Loyd. *The Parthian Shot.* New York: Viking Press, 1973.

Mailer, Norman. *Why Are We in Vietnam?* New York: G.P. Putnam's Sons, 1967.

Moore, Gene D. *The Killing at Ngo Tho.* New York: W.W. Norton, 1967.

Moore, Robin. *The Green Berets.* New York: Crown Publishers, 1965.

Morrison, C.T. *The Flame in the Icebox.* Jericho, N.Y.: Exposition, 1968.

Myers, Anton. *Once an Eagle.* New York: Holt, Rinehart & Winston, 1968.

O'Brien, Tim. *Going After Cacciato.* New York: Delacorte Press, 1978.

Pelfrey, William. *The Big V.* New York: Liveright, 1972.

Petrakis, Harry Mark. *In the Land of Mourning.* New York: McKay, 1973.

Rivers, G., and J. Hudson. *The Five Fingers.* New York: Doubleday, 1978.

Roth, Robert. *Sand in the Wind.* Boston: Little, Brown, 1973.

Sloan, James Park. *War Games.* Boston: Houghton Mifflin, 1971.

Stone, Robert. *Dog Soldiers.* Boston: Houghton Mifflin, 1974.

Webb, James H. *Fields of Fire.* New York: Prentice-Hall, 1978.

Werder, Albert. *A Spartan Education.* New York: Beekman, 1978.

Williams, John A. *Captain Blackman.* New York: Doubleday, 1972.

Wolfe, Michael. *Man on a String.* New York: Harper & Row, 1973.

Woods, William Crawford. *The Killing Zone.* New York: Harper's Magazine Press, 1970.

Personal narratives

Baker, Mark. *Nam.* New York: William Morrow, 1981.

Bergman, Lee, and James A. Daly. *A Hero's Welcome.* New York: Bobbs-Merrill, 1975.

Berrigan, Daniel. *Night Flight to Hanoi.* New York: Macmillan, 1968.

Bryan, C.D.B. *Friendly Fire.* New York: G.P. Putnam's Sons, 1976.

Caputo, Philip. *A Rumor of War.* Holt, Rinehart & Winston, 1977.

Denton, Jeremiah A. *When Hell Was in Session.* New York: Reader's Digest Press, 1976.

Downs, Frederick. *The Killing Zone: My Life in the Vietnam War.* New York: W.W. Norton, 1978.

Dudman, Richard. *Forty Days with the Enemy.* New York: Liveright, 1971.

Duncan, Donald. *The New Legions.* New York: Random House, 1967.

Elkins, Frank Callihan. *The Heart of a Man.* Edited by Marilyn Roberson Elkins. New York: W.W. Norton, 1973.

Emerson, Gloria. *Winners and Losers.* New York: Random House, 1976.

Glasser, Ronald J. *365 Days.* New York: George Braziller, 1971.

Halberstam, David. *The Making of a Quagmire.* New York: Random House, 1965.

Herr, Michael. *Dispatches.* New York: Alfred A. Knopf, 1977.

Kirk, Donald. *Tell It to the Dead: Memories of a War.* Chicago: Nelson-Hall, 1975.

Kovic, Ron. *Born on the Fourth of July.* New York: McGraw-Hill, 1976.

McCarthy, Mary. *The Seventeenth Degree.* New York: Harcourt Brace Jovanovich, 1974. Includes previously published pamphlets *Vietnam* (1967), *Hanoi* (1968), and *Medina* (1972).

Mailer, Norman. *The Armies of the Night.* New York: New American Library, 1968.

O'Brien, Tim. *If I Die in a Combat Zone.* New York: Delacorte Press, 1973.

Race, Jeffrey. *War Comes to Long An.* Berkeley: University of California Press, 1972.

Ross Martin. *Happy Hunting Ground.* New York: Atheneum, 1968.

Salisbury, Harrison E. *Behind-the-Lines — Hanoi.* New York: Harper & Row, 1967.

Santoli, Al. *Everything We Had.* New York: Random House, 1981.

Schell, Jonathan. *The Village of Ben Suc.* New York: Random House, 1967.

_____. *The Military Half.* New York: Alfred A. Knopf, 1968.

Sontag, Susan. *Trip to Hanoi.* New York: Farrar, Straus & Giroux, 1968.

Terzani, Tiziano. *Giai Phong!* New York: St. Martin's Press, 1976.

Thee, Marek. *Notes of a Witness: Laos and the Second Indochinese War.* New York: Random House, 1973.

Vance, Samuel. *The Courageous and the Proud.* New York: W.W. Norton, 1970.

Webb, Kate. *On the Other Side: 23 Days with the Viet Cong.* New York: Quadrangle Books, 1972.

Whitmore, Terry, as told to Richard Weber. *Memphis Nam Sweden: The Autobiography of a Black American Exile.* New York: Doubleday, 1971.

Young, Perry Deane. *Two of the Missing: A Reminiscence of Some Friends in the War.* New York: Coward, McCann & Geoghegan, 1975.

Critical literature

Beidler, Philip D. "Truth-Telling and Literary Values in the Vietnam Novel." *South Atlantic Quarterly* 78 (Spring 1979), pp. 141-56.

Bell, Pearl K. "Writing About Vietnam." *Commentary*, October 1978, pp. 74-77.

Bergonzi, Bernard. "Vietnam Novels: First Draft." *Commonweal*, October 27, 1972, pp. 84-88.

Grant, Zalin. "Vietnam as Fable." *The New Republic*, March 25, 1978, pp. 23-24.

Hellman, John. "The New Journalism and Vietnam: Memory as Structure in Michael Herr's *Dispatches.*" *South Atlantic Quarterly* 79 (Spring 1980), pp. 141-51. Reprinted in *Fables of Fact* (see below).

————. *Fables of Fact: The New Journalism as New Fiction.* Urbana: University of Illinois Press, 1981.

Jordan, C. "Vietnam Connection: New Novels." *Encounter*, Spring 1975, pp. 71-76.

Kazin, Alfred. "Vietnam: It was Us vs. Us." *Esquire*, March 1, 1978, pp. 120-23.

Klinkowitz, Jerome. *The American 1960s: Imaginative Acts in a Decade of Change.* Ames: Iowa State University Press, 1980.

McInerney, Peter. "Straight and Secret History in Vietnam War Literature." *Contemporary Literature* 22 (Spring 1981), pp. 187-204.

Maloff, Saul. "Vietnam Mon Amour." *Commonweal*, February 3, 1978, pp. 84-87.

Marin, Peter. "Coming to Terms with Vietnam." *Harper's*, December 1980, pp. 41-56.

Naparsteck, Martin J. "Vietnam War Novel." *Humanist*, July 1979, pp. 37-39.

Powers, T. "Vietnam in Fiction." *Commonweal*, March 15, 1974, pp. 39-41.

Roundy, Peter Edward. "Images of Vietnam: *Catch-22*, New Journalism, and the Postmodern Imagination." *Dissertation Abstracts International* 41:3111-A.

Saltzman, Arthur M. "The Betrayal of the Imagination: Paul Brodeur's *The Stunt Man* and Tim O'Brien's *Going After Cacciato*." *Critique*, 22 (I 1980), pp. 32-38.

Stromberg, Peter Leonard. "A Long War's Writing: American Novels About the Fighting in Vietnam Written While Americans Fought." *Dissertation Abstracts International* 35:4562-A.

Taylor, Gordon O. "American Personal Narrative of the War in Vietnam." *American Literature* 54 (May 1980), pp. 294-308.

_____. "Cast a Cold I: Mary McCarthy on Vietnam." *Journal of American Studies* 9 (April 1975), pp. 103-14.

Tetlow, Joseph A. "The Vietnam War Novel." *America*, July 1980, pp. 32-36.

Filmography

Narrative films

The Activist. Jana Film Enterprises, 1969. Directed by Art Napoleon.

Angels from Hell. Fanfare Film Productions, 1968. Directed by Bruce Kessler.

Apocalypse Now. United Artists, 1979. Directed by Francis Coppola.

The Boys in Company C. Columbia, 1978. Directed by Sidney Furie.

Captain Milkshake. Richmark Productions, 1970. Directed by Richard Crawford.

Coming Home. United Artists, 1978. Directed by Hal Ashby.

Cowards. Jaylo International Films, 1970. Directed by Simon Nuchtern.

The Deer Hunter. Universal, 1979. Directed by Michael Cimino.

Getting Straight. Columbia, 1970. Directed by Richard Rush.

Go Tell the Spartans. Avco Embassy, 1978. Directed by Ted Post.

The Green Berets. Warner Brothers, 1968. Directed by Ray Kellogg and John Wayne.

Greetings. West End Films, 1968. Directed by Brian De Palma.

Hail, Hero! Halcyon Productions, 1969. Directed by David Miller.

Heroes. Universal, 1977. Directed by Jeremy Paul Kagan.

Homer. Palomar Pictures International, 1970. Directed by John Trent.

I Feel It Coming. Sam Lake Enterprises, 1969. Directed by Sidney Knight.

The Losers. Fanfare Film Productions, 1970. Directed by Jack Starrett.

Medium Cool. Paramount, 1969. Directed by Haskell Wexler.

More American Graffiti. Universal, 1979. Directed by George Lucas.

The Quiet American. United Artists, 1958. Directed by Joseph L. Mankiewicz.

The Ravager. Green Dolphin Productions, 1970. Directed by Charles Nizet.

Rolling Thunder. American International, 1977. Directed by John Flynn.

Taxi Driver. Columbia, 1976. Directed by Martin Scorsese.

To the Shores of Hell. Crown International Pictures, 1966. Directed by Will Zens.

Tracks. Trio, 1977. Directed by Henry Jaglom.

Twilight's Last Gleaming. Allied Artists, 1977. Directed by Robert Aldrich.

Who'll Stop the Rain. United Artists, 1978. Directed by Karel Reisz.

A Yank in Vietnam. Allied Artists, 1964. Directed by Marshall Thompson.

Documentary films

A Face of War. Commonwealth United Entertainment, Inc., 1968. Directed by Eugene S. Jones.

For Life, Against the War. Film-Makers' Cooperative, 1968. Coordinated by Jules Rabin.

Hearts and Minds. Warner Brothers, 1975. Directed by Peter Davis.

High School. Osti Films, 1969. Directed by Frederick Wiseman.

Inside North Vietnam. Felix Greene, 1967. Directed by Felix Greene.

Mondo Bizarro. Olympic International Films, 1966. Directed by Seasu Hakasomi.

No Vietnamese Ever Called Me Nigger. Paradigm Films, 1968. Directed by David Loeb Weiss.

A Pilgrimage for Peace: Pope Paul VI Visits America. Roberts Productions, 1966. Directed by Carl Allensworth.

Quixote. Canyon Cinema Cooperative, 1965. Directed by Bruce Baillie.

Skezag. Soho Cinema, 1970. Directed by Joel Freedman and Philip F. Messina.

Sons and Daughters. American Documentary Films, 1967. Directed by Jerry Stoll.

23rd Psalm Branch. Brakhage, 1967. Directed by Stan Brakhage.

The War at Home. First Run Features, 1980. Directed by Glenn Silber and Barry Alexander Brown.

Secondary literature on the films

Adair, Gilbert. *Vietnam on Film.* New York: Proteus Books, 1981.

Auster, Al, and Leonard Quart. "Hollywood and Vietnam: The Triumph of the Will." *Cineaste* 9 (Spring 1979), pp. 4-9.

Axeen, D.; M. Dempsey; M. Kinder; E. Callenbach. "Four Shots at *The Deer Hunter.*" *Film Quarterly* 32 (Summer 1979), pp. 10-22.

Bogue, Ronald L. "The Heartless Darkness of *Apocalypse Now.*" *The Georgia Review* 35 (Fall 1981), pp. 611-26.

Corliss, R. "Guns and Buttered Popcorn: Vietnam Movies." *New Times,* March 20, 1978, pp. 65-68.

de Furia, R.D. "*Apocalypse Now*: The Ritual Murder of Art." *Western Humanities Review* 34 (Winter 1980), pp. 85-89.

Dempsey, M. "*Apocalypse Now.*" *Sight and Sound* 49 (Winter 1979-80), pp. 5-9.

Dickstein, Morris. "Bringing It All Back Home." *Partisan Review* 45 (4 1978), pp. 627-33.

Galperin, W. "History into Allegory: *The Wild Bunch* as Vietnam Movie." *Western Humanities Review* 35 (Summer 1981), pp. 165-72.

Gelman, D. "Vietnam Marches Home." *Newsweek,* February 13, 1978, pp. 85-86.

Gessner, P. "Films from the Vietcong." *Nation,* January 24, 1966, pp. 110-11.

Greenhouse, Lee. "Hollywood's Wartime Depiction of Vietnam." Harvard College Honors Thesis, 1978.

Grenier, R. "Coppola's Folly." *Commentary*, October 1979, pp. 67-73.

Kauffmann, S. "Tell the Real Lies: Films About Vietnam." *New Republic*, March 2, 1968, p. 26.

_____. "Hunting of the Hunters: Vietnam." *New Republic*, May 26, 1979, pp. 22-23.

Kelley, W.P. "*Apocalypse Now*: Vietnam as Generative Ritual," in *Rituals and Ceremonies in Popular Culture*, ed. by R.B. Browne. Bowling Green, Ohio: Bowling Green State University Press, 1980; pp. 192-205.

Kinder, M. "The Power of Adaptation in *Apocalypse Now*." *Film Quarterly* 33 (Winter 1979-80), pp. 12-20.

Kopkind, A. "Hollywood Politics: Hearts, Minds and Money." *Ramparts*, August 1975, pp. 45-48.

McInerney, Peter. "Apocalypse Then: Hollywood Looks Back at Vietnam." *Film Quarterly* 33 (Winter 1979-80), pp. 21-32.

Marin, Peter. "Coming to Terms With Vietnam." *Harper's*, December 1980, pp. 41-56.

Michaels, W.B. "Road to Vietnam." *MLN*, 94 (December 1979), pp. 1173-75.

Morrow, L. "Vietnam Comes Home: *Coming Home* and *The Deer Hunter*." *Time*, April 23, 1979, pp. 22-24.

Palmer, William J. "The Vietnam War Films." *Film Library Quarterly* 13 (4 1980), pp. 4-14.

Pym, John. "A Bullet in the Head: Vietnam Remembered." *Sight and Sound* 48 (Spring 1979), pp. 82-84.

_____. "*Apocalypse Now*: An Errand Boy's Journey." *Sight and Sound* 49 (Winter 1979-80), pp. 9-10.

Quart, Leonard. "Hollywood Discovers Vietnam." *USA Today*, May 1979, pp. 65-66.

Said, Lawrence. "The Making of *The Green Berets.*" *Journal of Popular Film* 6 (2 1977), pp. 106-25.

_____. "Hollywood and Vietnam." *Film Comment* 15 (September 1979), pp. 20-25.

Sayre, N. "At War in the Movies." *Progressive*, February 1980, pp. 51-54.

Siskel, Gene. "Hollywood Escalates Viet Nam War and the Conflict Is Booming." *The Chicago Tribune*, June 3, 1979.

Smith, Julian. "Between Vermont and Violence: Film Portraits of Vietnam Veterans." *Film Quarterly* 26 (Summer 1973), pp. 10-17.

_____. "Looking Away: Hollywood and Vietnam." *Progressive*, October 1975, pp. 58-59.

_____. *Looking Away: Hollywood and Vietnam.* New York: Charles Scribner's Sons, 1975.

Steele, R. "Felix Greene's *Inside North Vietnam.*" *Catholic World*, April 1968, pp. 24-30.

Sturken, Marita. "The Camera as Witness: Documentaries on the Vietnam War." *Film Library Quarterly* 13 (4 1980), pp. 15-20.

Tuch, Ronald. "Peter Davis' *Hearts and Minds.*" *Film Library Quarterly* 10 (1-2 1977), pp. 45-50.

Tuchman, Mitch. "Celluloid Vietnam." *New Republic*, May 31, 1975, pp. 28-30.

Turner, R. "Worst Years of Our Lives: Vietnam Movies." *New Times*, March 20, 1978, pp. 54-84.

Weiner, B. "*Hearts and Minds*: Full-Length Commercial Documentary of Vietnam." *Film Quarterly* 28 (Winter 1974), pp. 60-63.

Wood, Michael. "Bangs and Whimpers." *The New York Review of Books*, October 11, 1979, pp. 17-18.

Yurick, Sol. "*Apocalypse Now* / Capital Flow." *Cineaste* 10 (Winter 1979-80), pp. 21-23.

Index

A

Acheson, Dean, 16, 18
Advanced consumer capitalism, 71, 101
Agent Orange, 5
Allman, T.D., 25
Altman, Robert, *M*A*S*H*, 81
American Friends of Vietnam, 17
Ashby, Hal, *Coming Home*, 6, 79, 81, 83-84, 96
Aspegren, Chuck, 85
Auster, Al, 81, 84, 88

B

Baber, Asa, *The Land of a Million Elephants*, 41-42
Baker, Mark, *Nam*, 1, 43, 71
Ball, George, 24
Beidler, Philip D., 49
Bell, Pearl K., 45, 68
Binh Xuyen, 21
Bogue, Ronald L., 89, 90, 92, 93
Brando, Marlon, 93
Bryan, C.D.B., *Friendly Fire*, 6, 25, 26, 45, 71
Bundy, McGeorge, 24
Bunting, Josiah, *The Lionheads*, 48

C

Cable 1006, 30
Caputo, Philip, *A Rumor of War*, 5, 47, 50, 54, 61, 62-64, 70, 71, 98, 101, 102
Cazale, John, 85
Chomsky, Noam, *After the Cataclysm*, 2
CIA, 23, 24, 25, 38
Cimino, Michael, *The Deer Hunter*, 6, 79, 80, 81, 83-89, 96, 98
Clifford, Clark, 95
Conrad, Joseph, *Heart of Darkness*, 89, 90, 92, 93
Coppola, Francis, *Apocalypse Now*, 6, 7, 79, 83, 84, 88-94, 96, 98, 100
Country Joe and the Fish, 79
Cronkite, Walter, 33

D

Dai, Bao, 20, 21
Davis, George, *Coming Home*, 76-77, 100
Davis, Peter, *Hearts and Minds*, 7, 80, 94-96, 98, 100; *Hunger in America*, 94; *The Selling of the Pentagon*, 94
Democratic Republic of Vietnam (DRVN), 17, 18, 19, 24, 59
De Niro, Robert, 84
Dern, Bruce, 83
Devillers, Philippe, 4
Diem, Ngo Dinh, 20, 21, 22, 23, 24, 29, 30, 31, 37
Dien Bien Phu, 16, 18, 20, 54
Duc, Thich Quang, 23, 30
Dulles, John Foster, 11, 12, 16, 21
Durden, Charles, *No Bugles, No Drums*, 4, 5, 7, 27, 44, 48, 49-50, 71-72, 73-76, 98, 100
Duvall, Robert, 91
Dzundza, George, 85

E

Eastlake, William, *The Bamboo Bed*, 44, 48, 49, 54, 72, 97, 98, 100

Eisenhower, Dwight D., 11, 16, 17, 19, 21, 22
Ellsberg, Daniel, 95
Emerson, Gloria, 9; *Winners and Losers*, 3, 6, 8, 15, 16, 57, 71

F

Fall, Bernard, 4, 16, 19, 20, 29, 30, 33, 37
Fishel, Wesley, 21, 23
Fitzgerald, Frances, *Fire in the Lake*, 4, 6, 15, 19, 20, 21, 23, 25, 26, 29, 53
Flynn, John, *Rolling Thunder*, 81
Fonda, Jane, 77, 83-84
Ford, Gerald, 2
French in Vietnam, 10, 16, 17, 20, 29, 44, 53, 55
Fulbright, William, 95
Furie, Sidney, *The Boys in Company C*, 81

G

Gellhorn, Martha, 31
Geneva Conference, 18, 19, 20, 21, 22
Glasser, Ronald J., *365 Days*, 71
Graff, Gerald, *Literature Against Itself*, 27, 51, 101-102
Grant, Zalin, 9, 43, 63
Greene, Graham, 98; *The Quiet American*, 6, 8-14, 15, 16, 19, 20, 21, 27, 29, 37, 46, 55, 62, 66, 73, 80, 97
Groom, Winston, *Better Times Than These*, 39-40

H

Halberstam, David, 30, 33, 53, 60; *One Very Hot Day*, 5, 6, 54-56, 98; *The Making of a Quagmire*, 30
Haldeman, Joe W., *War Year*, 40-41
Harkins, Paul, 24
Hasford, Gustav, 102; *The Short-Timers*, 50

Heller, Joseph, *Catch-22*, 40-41, 44, 45, 50
Hellman, John, 45
Hendrix, Jimi, 92
Herr, Michael, *Dispatches*, 1, 5, 6, 8, 14, 26, 28-35, 36, 39, 43-52, 54, 62, 70, 88, 98, 99, 100, 101, 102
Hersh, Seymour, *My Lai 4*, 32
Hollywood and Vietnam, 79-96
Hope, Bob, 94
Hopper, Dennis, 81, 93
Huggett, William Turner, *Body Count*, 39-40

J

Jaglom, Henry, *Tracks*, 81-82
Johnson, Lyndon B., 22, 71
Jones, James, 39

K

Kagan, Jeremy Paul, *Heroes*, 81
Kai-shek, Chiang, 16, 17
Kempton, Murray, 32
Kennedy, John F., 17, 20, 24, 30, 63, 71, 98
Kennedy, Robert, 95
Khanh, Nguyen, 24
Khiem, Tran Thieu, 24
Knightley, Phillip, *The First Casualty*, 30, 32, 33, 53, 55
Kolpacoff, Victor, *The Prisoners of Quai Dong*, 5, 6, 63-65, 67, 68, 98
Kovic, Ron, *Born on the Fourth of July*, 5, 7, 54, 72-73, 98, 100, 102
Ky, Nguyen Kao, 24, 25

L

LaFeber, Walter, 3
Lansdale, Edward G., 19, 20, 21
Lasch, Christopher, 101-102; *The Culture of Narcissism*, 102
Last Patrol, 72
Lawrence, D.H., 86
Leibling, A.J., 14

Lewy, Guenter, *America in Vietnam*, 3
Lifton, Robert Jay, *Home from the War*, 71
Lindley, Richard, 33
Loan, Nguyen Ngoc, 33
Lodge, Henry Cabot, 24

M

McCarthy, Joseph, 16
MacLaine, Shirley, 94
Mailer, Norman, 39, 100; *Why Are We in Vietnam?*, 99; *The Armies of the Night*, 99
Maloff, Saul, 5
Mankiewicz, Joseph L., *The Quiet American*, 6, 80
Manning, Robert, 26
Mansfield, Mike, 17
Mao Tse-tung, 16
Marin, Peter, 2, 4, 6, 38, 68, 84, 88, 89, 93, 98
Marshal, George C., 18
Minh, Duong Van, 24, 37, 38
Minh, Ho Chi, 17, 18, 19, 37, 38, 39
Mohr, Charles, 31
Moore, Robin, *The Green Berets*, 5, 36-42
Morrison, Jim, 91, 100
Murphy, Audie, 80
Mus, Paul, 4
My Lai, 5, 32, 63

N

Nhu, Ngo Dinh, 23
Nixon, Richard M., 16, 17, 26, 32, 72, 95

O

O'Brien, Tim, *Going After Cacciato*, 5, 6, 54, 56-59, 62, 98; *If I Die in a Combat Zone*, 29, 59-60, 62
Operation Cedar Falls, 33-35
oss, 17

P

Palmer, William J., 82, 83, 85
Patti, Archimedes, *Why Viet Nam?*,
    17, 18, 19
Pentagon Papers, 18, 20, 26
"Pepsi Generation," 73
Perry, Merton, 31
Phat, Lam Van, 24
Porter, Gareth, *Vietnam: A History
    in Documents*, 18, 20
Post Vietnam Syndrome, 83
Pym, John, 82

Q

Quart, Leonard, 81, 84, 88

R

Redgrave, Michael, 80
Reisz, Karel, *Who'll Stop the Rain*,
    81, 82-83
Richardson, John, 23, 24
Rostow, Walt, 94, 95
Rusk, Dean, 24

S

Saltzman, Arthur M., 59
Santoli, Al, *Everything We Had*, 71
Savage, John, 84
Schell, Jonathan, *The Village of Ben
    Suc*, 33-35
Schneider, Bert, 94
Scorsese, Martin, *Taxi Driver*, 81
SEATO, 11, 20, 74
Sheen, Martin, 88, 91
Sinatra, Frank, 94
Sloan, James Park, *War Games*, 40-
    41

Smith, Walter Bedell, 19
South Vietnam, 3, 10, 12, 20, 31, 77,
    101
Spellman, Francis Cardinal, 20
Stone, I.F., 2
Stone, Robert, *Dog Soldiers*, 5, 6, 27,
    43, 63, 65-69, 73, 75-76, 82, 98,
    100, 101
Streep, Meryl, 87
Sully, François, 30
Sulzberger, "Punch," 30

T

Taylor, Gordon O., 9, 13
Tet Offensive, 3, 31, 32, 33
Tetlow, Joseph, 64
Thieu, Nguyen Van, 24, 25
"Throwaway society," 72, 75
Truman, Harry, 16, 17, 44, 95
Tse-tung, Mao, 16

V

Viet Cong, 5, 25, 26, 31, 33, 34, 37,
    39, 47, 55, 56, 62, 64, 75, 86, 89,
    92, 94
Viet Minh, 11, 12, 13, 16, 17, 18
Voigt, John, 77, 83-84

W

Wagner, Robert, 22
Walken, Christopher, 84
Watergate, 2
Watt, Ian, *Conrad in the Nineteenth
    Century*, 90
Wayne, John, 37; *The Green Berets*,
    80
Westmoreland, William, 3, 5, 18, 47,
    95